William Trant

Trade Unions

Their Origin and Objects, Influences, etc.

William Trant

Trade Unions
Their Origin and Objects, Influences, etc.

ISBN/EAN: 9783744662444

Printed in Europe, USA, Canada, Australia, Japan

Cover: Foto ©ninafisch / pixelio.de

More available books at **www.hansebooks.com**

TRADE UNIONS

THEIR ORIGIN AND OBJECTS, INFLUENCE
AND EFFICACY

BY

WILLIAM TRANT

"This that they call Organization of Labour is the Universal Vital Problem of the World. It is the problem of the whole future for all who will in future pretend to govern men."—THOMAS CARLYLE.

LONDON
KEGAN PAUL, TRENCH & CO., 1, PATERNOSTER SQUARE

1884

✳   ✳
✳

THE following chapters are based upon the Essay, for which the author obtained the £50 prize offered at the Trade Unions Congress in 1873 by the late Mr. Alexander Macdonald, M.P. Much new information and the latest statistics have been added to the work as it appeared in its original form. The author is indebted to the secretaries of the leading Trade Unions and to others, for information and assistance in producing the book, and their kind services are acknowledged in the text.

NOTE.—While the following pages were passing through the press (July, 1884) an unfortunate dispute arose at Burnley between the weavers and their employers, which renders it necessary to modify the allusion on page 53 to the "Amalgamation of the Northern Counties Association."

CONTENTS.

———◦◇◦———

CHAPTER I.

HISTORICAL SKETCH.

PAGE

Serfdom—Emancipation—The domestic system—The "capitalist craftsman"—The working class—The first crisis—
The statutes of labourers—The black death—High wages,
cheap food, and short hours—Combination—Guilds—The
first union—Rise of the artisan—The Lollards—Antagonism of the wealthy—The peasants' revolt—Oppression of
the working classes—Debasement of the coin—Confiscation
of the guilds—Combination laws—The poor laws—Continued decline of the workman—His miserable condition
in the nineteenth century—Trade unions—Their original
rules—Combinations of employers   1

CHAPTER II.

TRADE UNIONS—THEIR PROGRESS AND DEVELOPMENT.

Attempts to crush unionism—Hornby v. Close—Combination
made legal—First conference of union delegates—The
Sheffield outrages—The Royal Commission—Unequal laws
—Picketing—The Trade Union Acts   34

CHAPTER III.

TRADE UNIONS—THEIR OBJECTS.

Equality of bargaining power—To raise wages—Protection—
Sick benefits, etc.—Mutual support—Moral improvement
of the workman—Constitution of a union—The Amalgamated Society of Engineers—Executive of unions prevents

PAGE

strikes—Unselfishness of unionism—Trade unions congresses—Their influence—The International—The Paris
conference—Trade councils in New Zealand 43

CHAPTER IV.

TRADE UNIONS—THEIR EFFICACY.

They have raised wages—Proofs and instances—How much
have the unions raised wages?—The unions a record of the
state of the labour market—Wages would not rise quickly
but for unions—"An unsuccessful strike often succeeds"—
Local strikes affect distant areas and many trades—The
agricultural labourers—Where unionism is weak, wages
are low—Shorter hours, yet more work—Piece-work—
Errors of unions—Difficulties of the union secretary—Foolish strikes injurious, may prevent a rise of wages—A fair
day's wages—Employers' combinations—Boards of arbitration—Trade unions prevent strikes—Spread of unionism—
The power of trade unions acknowledged by the employers
—Trade unions as friendly and benefit societies—Women's
trade unions—Other features of trade unions, some obsolete
—Proceedings of unions should be public 67

CHAPTER V.

TRADE UNIONS—THEIR INFLUENCE.

Effects of high wages—Desire to retain a high social standard
—Well-paid labour remunerative to the capitalist—Foreign
competition—High wages does not mean high prices—The
high price of coal and the colliers—Socialism—Co-operation—Trade unions stimulate invention—Expenditure by
the working classes—Advantages of shorter hours—Self-
improvement—Moral influence of trade unions—Endeavour
to make good workmen—Educational influences of trade
unions—Political influence—Future of trade unions—Legal
requirements — Class distinctions — Good conduct of
unionists insisted upon—Mutual assistance—The union
offices storehouses of statistics—The British Association
on trade unions—Recapitulation and conclusion ... 126

INDEX 183

TRADE UNIONS.

THEIR ORIGIN AND OBJECTS, INFLUENCE AND EFFICACY.

———◦◦◦———

CHAPTER I.

HISTORICAL SKETCH.

Serfdom—Emancipation—The domestic system—The "capitalist craftsman"—The working class—The first crisis—The statutes of labourers—The black death—High wages, cheap food, and short hours—Combination—Guilds—The first union—Rise of the artisan—The Lollards—Antagonism of the wealthy—The peasants' revolt—Oppression of the working classes—Debasement of the coin—Confiscation of the guilds—Combination laws—The poor laws—Continued decline of the workman—His miserable condition in the nineteenth century—Trade unions—Their original rules—Combinations of employers.

THOSE who so often speak of the "welfare of the State" would do well to remember that the phrase has never yet meant the "welfare of the people." The "good old times" were good only for a small portion

of the community, and although year after year has
shown constant improvement, yet that amelioration has
been very slow and lamentably imperfect. Aristotle
says, in his "Politics," that the best and most perfect
commonwealth is one which provides for the happiness
of *all* its members. The fact that the great philosopher
conceived such a noble sentiment so long ago is in itself
remarkable; but admiration for his wisdom is somewhat diminished when it is found that, "although
artisans and trades of every kind are necessary to a
State, they are not parts of it," and their happiness,
therefore, is of a kind with which the "best and most
perfect commonwealth" has no concern whatever. "The
same law must be for all classes of my subjects," said
Henry II., but labourers were not considered subjects.
So late as Elizabeth's time they were spoken of (by
Shakespeare) as "fragments." Even the Magna Charta,
of which Englishmen are so justly proud, referred but
to a moiety of the two millions of persons who inhabited
England at the time of its promulgation. It affected
freemen alone, and there is little doubt that nearly one-
half of the entire population was then in a state of
slavery so abject that, in the language of the old law-
writers, "the villein knew not in the evening what he
was to do in the morning, but he was bound to do
whatever he was commanded." He was liable to beat-
ing, he was incapable of acquiring property for himself, and any he got became his master's; he could be
separated from his wife and children, and sold to
another lord, or he could be passed with the land upon
which he lived, as if he had been a chattel attached
to it.

Various causes noiselessly and gradually effaced this

miserable condition, though at a very slow rate. "Faint traces of it," says Lord Macaulay, "were detected by the curious, so late as the days of the Stuarts; nor has that institution [villenage], even to this hour, been abolished by statute." From the earliest times, however, serfdom in England bore within it the germs of its own destruction. The lord might enfranchise his villein, or the latter could purchase his freedom. If, too, the slave escaped to some town, and remained there unclaimed a year and a day, he became a free man. There were also difficulties in the way of proving villenage, the onus of which proof always lay with the lord, while in all disputes on the subject the presumption of law was in favour of liberty. "Thus," writes Creasy, "while at the period when we first can assert the common law of the complete English nation to commence, we find this species of slavery so widely established in this country, we also find the law for its gradual and ultimately certain extinction." The Church, too, discountenanced slavery. Theodore denied Christian burial to the kidnapper, and prohibited the sale of children by their parents after the age of seven. Violation of the prohibition was punished with excommunication. The murder of a slave by his owner, though no crime in the eye of the State, became a sin for which penance was exacted by the Church. The slaves attached to Church property were freed, and manumission became frequent in wills, as the clergy taught that such a gift was a boon to the soul of the dead.

With half a nation in slavery there could be no "working class," as the term is generally understood. The wealthy kept domestic artisans amongst their servants, and the wants of the nobles were almost entirely supplied by their retainers. The villeins tilled the soil, while the men in towns worked on what is now called the " domestic system." The factory system and the capitalist employer were not yet known, and the employers of labour were those who provided materials which they hired men to work into the articles required. The glazier glazed, but did not find the glass ; the black-smith forged, but did not find the iron. There was, therefore, very little hiring of labourers. "The capi-talist employer," says Professor Thorold Rogers in " Six Centuries of Labour and Wages," " the first middle man, is entirely unknown till the seventeenth century ; and the capitalist purchaser of raw material, the second middle man, is later still in the economy of society." At a very early date, however, craftsmen became the chief purchasers of the materials on which they worked, and the "capitalist artisan " developed considerably in the sixteenth century. The London tailors, even in the reign of Edward III., were the great importers of woollen cloths, and there can be no doubt that at this time many of the craftsmen traded in the raw materials which they worked. As, however, the trades became more prosperous, and the poor, who flocked to the towns, more numerous, the traders gradually ceased working at their craft, and, confining themselves to trading, left the manual labour to their less fortunate companions. That is to say, a class of small dealers in raw material sprang into existence. The distinction of classes became marked. The shoemaker soon learnt to look down upon the cobbler, and the leather merchant to despise the shoemaker.

The " full history of our nation," it is agreed, begins

in the reign of Henry II., and it is thenabouts that we
find anything like a working class gathering itself together. In the three centuries which immediately
succeeded the Norman conquest, the commerce of England was greatly extended. Foreign commodities were
"introduced in abundance, and native manufactures
established and improved." This naturally attracted to
the towns such serfs as wished for liberty, and thus we
find springing up in the towns a class of men possessed
of personal freedom, but destitute of property in land.
These were the forerunners of the working class. The
Statute of Labourers (23 Ed. III., c. 1) clearly shows
the existence of a wages-receiving class, the remuneration being about one penny a day in addition to food;
and when it is remembered that the sum mentioned was
sufficient to purchase a couple of fowls or the fifth part
of a sheep, it is evident that the recipients were well off
as things went. Indeed, the statute referred to was
passed because, in the opinion of the landholders, the
wages of agricultural labourers had become "excessive."
Here was, in fact, the first "crisis" on record between
employers and employed in England. The depopulation
(amounting, it is said, to one-third of the nation) which
followed the great plague of 1348, the "Black Death,"
caused a natural rise in the price of labour. Whole
villages died out; houses fell in ruins; entire flocks
perished for want of herdsmen; and the corn crops
perished for want of reapers. The clergy even raised
their fees for masses and prayers, because fewer persons
were able to afford such luxuries; merchants and
tradesmen took advantage of the small supply of wares
to raise their prices; and in like manner the workmen
endeavoured to profit by the dearth of labour, by refus-

ing to work except at enormous prices. The wealthy class objected to all this, and the purpose of the Act re-referred to was to fix the wages, by requiring all labourers, etc., to accept the same remuneration as had been customary before the plague. Any lord of the manor paying more was to be mulcted in treble damages; food was to be sold at reasonable prices; and alms were forbidden to able-bodied labourers. The statute, however, seems to have been disregarded; and two years later we find the master shearmen of London complaining to the city authorities that they could not get men at the same wages as formerly, and that the workmen also refused to work unless they were paid by the piece. There had, indeed, already been something of the nature of a "strike," and it was therefore ordered that any further disputes should be settled by the warden of the trade. If a workman did not submit, he was to be punished by the mayor and aldermen. All, however, was of no avail, and what is alone surprising is the obtuseness that could for a moment imagine the Act could be enforced. The statute had to be enforced by the Manor Court, and that court depended for efficiency upon the good will existing between landlord and tenant; and where statute prices were paid the difference was made up in some other way. Professor Rogers has recently brought to light some curious instances of evasions of the Act, by the alterations in the record of the court from the price actually paid to the statute prices; alterations evidently made to technically conform to the law, while actually evading it. At last the peasants combined to resist the law. They organized themselves; and they subscribed con-siderable sums of money for the defence and protection of serfs, which, it has been suggested, may have included the payment of fines. In point of fact, here is a rudimentary trade union to resist an unjust law and to secure higher wages. A similar statute to the one above quoted was passed in 1362, when, after a violent tempest, a royal order was issued that the materials for roofing and the wages of tilers should not be enhanced by reason of the damage done by the storm. An additional statute, with a similar object, was passed the following year.

From these sources, and from the industrious researches of Professor Thorold Rogers, we learn what were the wages earned at the period before the rise set in. It will be sufficient to say here that they were not satisfactory, though not so meagre as has been generally supposed. The Acts, however, were disregarded, the men refusing to work for less than double or treble the sums prescribed by statute. For about a dozen years wages continued to rise, until in 1363 the prosperity of the peasantry was so great that an Act (37 Edward III., c. 14) was passed enjoining carters, ploughmen, and farm servants generally, not to eat or drink "excessively," or to wear any cloth except "blanket and russet wool of twelvepence," while domestic servants were declared to be entitled to only one meal a day of flesh and fish, and were to content themselves at other meals with "milk, butter, cheese, and other such victuals." * These restrictions were as futile as those which preceded them, and it would be foolish to weary the reader with an account of similar legislation effected during the succeeding century, in

* In Scotland, at a much later date, farm labourers complained that they had to eat salmon more than four days a week.

spite of which, however, wages constantly advanced; and we find an Act passed in the reign of Richard II. stating that labourers would not work except at a rate "much more than hath been given to such servants and labourers in any time past." Indeed, they were the halcyon days of the British labourer. He was much better off then than he is now. The rise in the wages of labour after the famine of Edward II. was as much as from twenty-three per cent. to thirty per cent.; and after the Black Death in the following reign the average advance was upwards of fifty per cent. more. The masons succeeded in obtaining an advance of sixty per cent., the reason of which will be given immediately. Great, too, as was the rise in wages, there was no corresponding rise in the price of provisions. Everything the labourer needed was as cheap as it ever had been, his labour was rising in value week by week, and he worked only eight hours a day. Never before or since have the working men of England been so well off as far as material comforts were concerned, and this halcyon period lasted until 1390. It will be necessary further on to trace the reasons of the downward tendency that began to show itself in that year; and to show how it was that labourers who had become masters of the situation were again degraded to the level of serfs. It would be interesting to inquire whether any "union" or "combination" had given the men strength to resist the injustice which the Acts just mentioned inflicted upon them by curbing the "aspiring exertions of industry and independency." Materials upon which to found a decided opinion are, unfortunately, very scarce. One thing, however, is certain. The people of England had long been familiar with the principle of association for trade and other purposes. Even so early as the time of Canute, associations under the name of "guilds" were established for religious purposes. Similar brotherhoods afterwards developed into combinations of merchants for mutual assistance and protection, and were followed in the fourteenth century by "craft-guilds," which, as their name implies, were unions of handicraftsmen—the principal guild being that of the weavers. The very essence of the guilds was mutual support, mutual protection, and mutual responsibility. They were, indeed, the first friendly societies. These guilds gradually extended their influence beyond the limits of particular trades, and ultimately became far more powerful than the municipal corporations of the present day. The notions of the members of the guilds were of a very exclusive nature in regard to the admission of members. No villeins were permitted to join them, and all freemen who were proposed had to be duly elected. The noblest of all the guilds of the Middle Ages was undoubtedly that of the masons. This brotherhood arose from the circumstances in which the travelling builders of the Middle Ages found themselves placed. "They were brought together from distant homes to be employed for a considerable time on such great works as our mediæval churches and cathedrals. Near the rising structure on which they were engaged it was necessary. that they should provide for themselves a common shed or tabernacle." This was the original masons' "lodge." Before all things it was necessary that masons should be "free and accepted." The entrance into this guild, as indeed into all others, was, in accordance with the spirit of the times, surrounded by mysterious rites and ceremonies, and all such societies had their peculiar lore and traditions. Their original intentions have long ago been disregarded. All that remains of the masons' guild is the now fashionable order of "Freemasons," and of the others the rich livery companies of London and the guilds of elsewhere, who now spend their dying moments, as they inaugurated their existence centuries ago, at dinner.* The exclusiveness of the guilds naturally separated still more the incipient working class from their well-to-do superiors, and tended more and more to give the workmen separate views and interests, which were not infrequently antagonistic to those of the master. When two or three are gathered with identical interests (and those interests opposed to the wishes of their employers, who are already combined), it seems so natural for them to form a combination of some sort or other that it is impossible to resist the belief that in the fourteenth century the working man—excluded from the guild—would unite with his fellows, if not for general, yet for specific objects in connection with his condition. It is gratifying to learn that this view is taken by so high an authority as Dr. Lujo Brentano, who also points out that, at about the time referred to, accounts of "strikes in the building trade are particularly numerous;" and there is in existence a "royal mandate as to the workmen who have withdrawn from the palace at Westminster." Indeed, it is beyond dispute that the masons of the fourteenth century maintained a higher rate of wages than was paid to other crafts, as has been above mentioned, solely on

* It is gratifying to find that now some of the livery companies are devoting a portion of their funds to useful purposes, such as the promotion of technical education, etc.

account of the combination these artisans were able to effect; a fact that non-unionists of to-day would do well to remember. This view is strengthened by the fact that in 1383 the authorities of the city of London issued a proclamation forbidding all "congregations, covins, and conspiracies of workmen;" and four years later three shoemakers were carried off to Newgate for violating it; while in 1396 a similar coalition of saddlers was suppressed. Two laws also were enacted against combinations, congregations, and chapters of workmen (which had been established to limit the number of working hours), viz., the 34 Edward IV., c. 9, and 3 Henry VI., c. 1. The punishments inflicted upon working men for combining were very severe, and yet they combined in spite of such punishments. The endeavours of the labourers to raise wages showed themselves most prominently in the trades in which, as in the cloth manufactures, development was most rapidly progressing, and in which there existed a large working class.

The prosperity of the labourers and artisans produced events that alarmed the privileged classes. The emancipation of the serfs had for some time past proceeded very rapidly, from causes which have been already indicated. Professor Thorold Rogers, after an enormous amount of research, writes of the fourteenth century, "In the many thousands of bailiffs and manor rolls which I have read, I have never met with a single instance of the sale of a serf, nor have I discovered any labour rent for which an equitable money payment could not be substituted." Indeed, during the reign of Edward II., the practice became general of accepting money compensation in lieu of labour rents; and at

the end of a quarter of a century the rule had become
almost universal. The improvement in the condition
of the serfs created an amount of independence among
them that had the happiest results. Sir Robert Sale,
Captain-General of Norwich in 1381, was the son of a
villein, was born a serf, as was also Grostête, the great
Oxford scholar of the thirteenth century, thus showing
that even in those days serfs could rise to very high
positions. There is abundant evidence, too, that they
became possessed of property, and indeed, as they became enfranchised, they also became copyholders. It is
certain they paid rent, which indicates a real bargain
between the lord and the serf which the former could
not break if the other satisfied his dues; and he could
recover wages due to him from his lordly employer by
distraint upon his goods, even upon his chattels, and
therefore could not be a chattel himself. The impetus
given to this process by the general rise after the
Black Death was brief, and that plague, in short,
emancipated almost the whole of the surviving serfs.

It was therefore amongst a prosperous and independent class that Wiklif's "Poor Priests," or Lollards,
followed by John Ball, also a priest, preached doctrines
that in those days were revolutionary doctrines, and,
in the eyes of some people, are so still. From village
to village the old couplet was repeated:

> "When Adam delved and Eve span,
> Who was then the gentleman?"

The people were taught that those who laboured, did
so not only for themselves, but to enable others to live
without labour, or to live by mischievous labour. The
"equality" expounded in the Bible was explained to

them, and generally it was impressed upon them that they were oppressed by a privileged class whom accident, fraud, or force had placed in a superior social sphere. The men were not starving, and had time to listen and to think, and above all things to combine. And they did combine. They subscribed money; they shielded the escaped serf from the pursuit of his lord; *Stile* the serf and the free joined in a common cause, and waited but the signal to "strike" against their enemies. The sign was at length given, and the result was, on the 10th of June, 1381, the Peasants' Revolt, or Wat Tyler's Rebellion. This was a rising caused, not by the outrage on Tyler's daughter, or even the poll tax, but by the general attempts by the upper classes to force down the wages of the labourers of England, and to take from them the rights they had won, though of course other grievances would not be forgotten. In all risings for a particular object, the opportunity is seized of making many demands. For the particulars of that revolt the reader is referred to the history of the period. The rebellion nearly succeeded, but the labourers were cajoled into quietude.

From this time forward for three centuries the history of the labouring class is a sad story. The governing powers never forgave the Lollards, nor those who listened to them. They seized every opportunity of crushing the people, and it is only recently that policy has been departed from. It is not too much to say that from this time to 1824, in the words of the author already quoted, "a conspiracy concocted by the law and carried out by parties interested in its success, was entered into to cheat the English workman of his wages, to tie him to the soil, to deprive him of age, and to degrade him into irreparable poverty." The first of these repressive measures was the debasement of the coin by Henry VIII. and the guardians of Edward VI. The nefarious transactions by which this was brought about had for their object the replenishment of the royal coffers out of the earnings of the artisans and labourers, and they succeeded in that object. The peasantry were already impoverished by the action of the landowners in substituting sheep-farming for agriculture, and the new state of affairs oppressed them with great severity. The purchasing power of the revenue fell to one-third of its original capacity, and the consequent rise in prices was one and a half. In other words, if wages rose from 6d. to 9d. a day, the labourer had to pay 3s. for meat, 2s. 5d. for bread, and 2s. 6d. for butter and cheese, where he had paid 1s. before. This, it is obvious, put back the labourer into a position of penury to which he had not been accustomed, and to which he did not readily submit. His condition was again almost that of the serf. From childhood to old age all was labour. Eight hours no longer constituted a day's work. His miserable condition was rendered worse by the dissolution of the monasteries that accompanied the debasement of the coin. A great part of the vast funds of the monasteries was devoted to the relief of the poor, and to their assistance in many ways. When this was withdrawn, no substitute was provided in its place. These transactions were followed by the confiscation of the property of the guilds. I have described them as the first Friendly Societies. The guilds assisted the artisan in times of difficulty, allowed him loans without interest, and granted benefits to his widow. The effect of the confiscation of the guilds was the same as would result from the confiscation of the funds of the Friendly Societies; and it is worth noting, as an argument in favour of strong union, that only the provincial guilds were molested, those in London being so powerful that the Crown dared not molest them.

The working men resisted these oppressions, and vigorous measures were passed to force them into submission. An Act was passed in the reign of Edward VI., which shows pretty plainly what was thought in those days of the "working classes." If a man refused to work at statute prices he was branded with the letter V (vagabond), and reduced to slavery for two years. If he attempted to escape from that condition he was branded with S, and became a slave for life; and if he objected to that state he was hanged. It is also evident that the spirit of combination was growing amongst the labourers and artisans, for the laws against workmen's combinations were made still more stringent than hitherto. The preamble of 2nd and 3rd Edward VI., cap. 15 (A.D. 1548), set forth that "artificers, handicraftsmen, and labourers had made confederacies and promises, and have sworn mutual oaths, not only that they should not meddle with one another's work, and perform and finish what another hath begun; but also to constitute and appoint how much they shall do in a day, and what hours and times they shall work, contrary to the laws and statutes of this realm, and to the great impoverishment of his Majesty's subjects." Any one convicted for the third time of having joined such a combination had his ear cut off, and altogether the punishments were very severe. It may be gathered, then, that the principle of combination amongst the workpeople was rapidly progressing, and was met under the Tudors and Stuarts in a spirit which, it is to be regretted, is not wholly extinct at the present day, as recent events have shown.

It is not surprising that this state of affairs should have impressed the thinking minds of the period; and that the causes and remedies should be considered. Statesmen and persons of influence began to acknowledge the justice of the demands of the workpeople. In Sir Thomas More's *Utopia* the great statesman advocates almost all the reforms that have taken place since his day, and many that have not yet been accomplished. Indeed, as Mr. J. R. Green points out, " In his treatment of the question of labour he still remains far in advance of current opinion. The whole system of society around him seemed to him 'nothing but a conspiracy of the rich against the poor.' Its economic legislation was simply the carrying out of such a conspiracy by process of law. The rich are ever striving to pare away something further fron the daily wages of the poor by private fraud, and even by public law, so that the wrong already existing (for it is a wrong that those from whom the State derives most benefit should receive least reward) is made yet greater by means of the law of the State. The rich devise every means by which they may in the first place secure to themselves what they have amassed by wrong, and then take to their own use and profit at the lowest possible price the work and labour of the poor." The result was the wretched existence to which the labour class was doomed—" a life so wretched that even a beast's life seems enviable." More then gives his remedies. The end of labour alws, he says, should be the welfare of the labourer. Labour should be compulsory with all.

Unless a man work neither shall he eat. Even in those days, 1516, More demanded that the period of toil should be shortened to nine hours, with a view to the intellectual improvement of the worker: there must be also, he pleaded, "a public system of education," comfortable homes for the people, complete toleration and equality of all religions, and much more in the same strain. I do not suppose that any book that was ever written has done so much for the working classes as the *Utopia*, written by the proposer of the nine hours system more than three hundred years ago. The general progress of civilisation, even, had its drawbacks as regards the humbler classes. The general diffusion of the art of printing, the great geographical discoveries effected in the sixteenth century, and the general activity which prevailed throughout Europe immediately after the Reformation, gave a great stimulus to trade and commerce, the effects of which were long felt. This, of course, had a beneficial influence. It had however, some drawbacks. Amongst them may be mentioned that in the seventeenth century the practice of setting children prematurely to work prevailed to a very large extent. At Norwich, the chief seat of the clothing trade, children began to work at six years old, and earned not the "insignificant trifle" which was paid to the little sufferers forty years ago, but very much more than was necessary for their own sustenance. In the opposition which was shown at the time to this inhumanity is to be discerned the dawn of the Factory Acts, and of the opposition which was subsequently offered by Trade Unions to the overworking of youths and children.

I must mention another kind of legislation that emphasized the evils already indicated. A state of

c

affairs had been produced which created a class who
required not only work, but food, and it was sought to
remedy the evil by the enactment of poor laws. I must
refer the reader elsewhere for an account of statutes
whose chief result was the manufacture of paupers, and
whose only effect could be to make the poor poorer.
It will be sufficient to say here that the Justices in
quarter sessions had the power to fix wages, a power
that continued under legal sanction till 1812. Naturally they were fixed at the lowest possible figure, the
Justices knowing full well that any deficiency would be
paid out of the poor rates, to which all occupiers—that
is, the country at large—would be obliged to contribute.
There could be but one result from this. Wages would
continually fall, and the amount of poor relief as continually rise. As a consequence the time would ultimately arrive when it would require the whole of the
rent from land in order to relieve the poor. Indeed,
that condition was being approached and would undoubtedly have been reached but for the discovery of
steam power and machine weaving, which, as will
appear later on, created a great demand for labour,
and raised wages.

In spite of all these difficulties, however, the men
continued to combine, and the legislature to pass laws
against combination. The revolution of 1688 gave no
liberties to the artisans and the peasants. In the
sixteenth and seventeenth centuries it was ordained
that "journeymen should make no unlawful assemblies,
brotherhoods, congregations, and flockings together."
The Act of 2 and 3 Ed. VI., c. 15 (see *ante*, p. 15) was
confirmed by 22–23 Charles II., and remained in force
until repealed by 6 Geo. IV., c. 129. The stringent

laws, too, to which working men were subjected after
the Restoration, rendered their position far from comfortable or just. As if the statutes were not sufficiently
rigorous, the construction of the existing laws, the
offence of conspiracy, originally referring only to combinations for the purpose of procuring false evidence, or
of committing some crime, was extended to associations
of workmen whose purpose was to raise wages. Even
so late as the end of the last century the farm labourer
had no right to sell his labour in the best market, but
was compelled to work for any employer in his parish
who chose to demand his services at a price fixed by
statute. It was not until 1795 that a workman could
legally travel in search of employment out of his own
parish. In 1545 the City of London complained that
the importation of foreign manufactures was ruining the
country, and demanded low wages as a remedy. In 1680
there was, as there is now, the cry that if we paid our
artisans high wages we should be unable to compete
with foreign countries. In that year Mr. John Bassett,
the member for Barnstaple, remarked that it was impossible for our textures to maintain a competition with
the produce of the Indian looms. "An English
mechanic," he said, "instead of slaving like a native of
Bengal for a piece of copper, exacted a shilling a day."
Although this amount is equivalent to only about one-
half of the present rate of wages, there were even then,
as indeed there always have been, attempts to reduce
the amount; and there is ample evidence that so long
ago as when the above words were spoken there was
"the vehement and bitter cry of labour against capital."
"For so miserable a recompense," wrote Lord Macaulay
on the aforesaid one shilling a day, "were the pro-

ducers of wealth compelled to toil, rising early and
lying down late, while the master clothier, eating,
sleeping, and idling, became rich by their exertions."
From the earliest times until the present day, then,
employers have endeavoured to pay their men as little
as possible for as many hours' work as they could
possibly get out of them. In this task the masters have
ever been assisted by a Parliament composed of sympathizing friends—a Parliament which has always yielded
reluctantly to any measure calculated to improve the
masses, but has greedily accepted any proposal to
benefit the few at the cost of the many; and although
the onward and upward march of civilization has rendered such conduct less easy in the present day, yet
still there is the old tendency to legislate as though
the capitalist were entitled to all the plums and the
labourer to all the kicks.

The numerous attempts to fix wages by Act of
Parliament were nearly all failures. The assessment of
weavers' wages by the Justices had fallen into disuse
before 1720. In that year the Justices reasserted the
authority they possessed, and fixed wages, but their
injunctions were disregarded. So late as 1768 an Act
was passed compelling the London tailors to work from
six a.m. to seven p.m., with an interval of one hour only
for refreshments. The same Act also fixed the wages
of the clothworker at 2s. 7d. a day. Either master or
servant was liable to imprisonment for two months for
violating these rules; and a master was further liable
to a fine of £500 if he employed workmen who lived
more than five miles from London. In 1795 the Berkshire magistrates at Speenhamland declared that wages
should rise or fall with the price of bread, and them-

selves fixed the rates. Numerous Acts were passed
about this time regulating, or rather interfering with,
the most minute details of manufacturing industry. To
stimulate the Macclesfield trade it was enacted that no
"buttons or button-holes made of cloth, serge, drugget,
frieze, camlet, or any other stuffs, should be made, set,
or bound on clothes, or worn;" and the bare enumera-
tion of similar legislation would occupy more space
than is at present at disposal. The attempts to keep
wages down were supported by statesmen who ought
to have known better. Pitt, Fox, and Whitbread
distinctly asserted the unjust and pernicious doctrine
that a labourer's remuneration should be proportioned,
not to his services, but to his wants, and in 1796 the
magistrates in Berkshire attempted to "settle the
incomes of the industrious poor." The liberty of operatives was still further restricted at the close of the
eighteenth century, by an Act of Parliament which
declared to be illegal, all contracts, except between
masters and men, for obtaining advances of wages,
altering the usual time of working, decreasing the
quantity of work.

It is difficult to conceive, in the face of all this, how
the condition of the working man has improved in the
slightest degree. Indeed, it has not increased pro-
portionally. He has certainly been enveloped, so to
speak, in the general progress of affairs; he has doubtless shared somewhat in the national prosperity; but
whatever improvement has taken place in the condition
of the working classes, does not at all correspond with
the improvement which has taken place in the middle
and upper classes. In regard to the agricultural
labourer the case is very bad. In 1740 a Suffolk

labourer could buy for 5s., what in 1801 cost him
26s. 5d. As Professor Rogers says, "For five centuries
and a half, for fifteen, sixteen generations, there was no
appreciable alteration in the condition of the people."
It remained stationary, where it did not deteriorate,
from Henry III. to George III. The condition to-day
of the labourer in the agricultural districts of England,
and the instances which are reported of the conduct of
the masters, speak of misery and oppression worthy of
the Tudors and the Stuarts, or at any rate of that time
when Sir Robert Hazlewood propounded the peculiar
notions of justice which then occupied the brains of men
of "rank and family," and for which notions, Heaven
knows, there was ample room in the repository referred
to. Down to 1779 the condition of the miners in Scotland was literally one of serfdom. They were obliged
to remain in the pit as long as the owner chose to keep
them there, and they were actually sold as part of the
capital invested in the work. If they took work elsewhere their master could always have them fetched back
and flogged as thieves for having robbed him of their
labour. It is no wonder that in 1745 the magistrates of
Lancashire were alarmed at the symptoms of combination and disaffection, and once again resorted to an
attempt to fix wages in spite of past experiences.

It were tedious to mention the various events which
have ruffled the career of the labourer during the last
century. It is often stated that wages had gradually
risen and food had cheapened. This, however, is a
mistake. From 1800 until after the repeal of the
Corn Laws the state of the labourer seems never to
have been in its natural condition. During that period
wages were never high, and at times the distress was

very great. England was then (1810–1812) in anything but an enviable position. On the Continent the hand of every nation was against her, and her hand was against every nation. She was at war with all the empires she had not subsidized in the Old World, and her arms were struggling with her own offspring in the New World, as well as fighting a war of oppression in the Indies. These wars, which lasted for a quarter of a century, spread misery like a pall over the land. Trade was paralyzed; foreign ports, both in Europe and America, were closed to us, and by a pigheaded policy * our ports were closed to them. There was not work for anybody, and nearly everybody, therefore, was starving. Just at this time an event took place which, although a great blessing, and known to be so at the time by far-sighted men, was not unaccompanied by those disasters which generally accompany great changes. While nearly all men were out of work, capitalists began to introduce into the manufacturing districts labour-saving machines, which dispensed with seven out of every eight hand-workers. This was the last straw. The men were in no humour for reasoning on the principles of political economy. They were starving; and to their eyes the new machinery cut off every chance of their ever working again. They formed the strongest and most secret combination ever known in this country. Their object was to destroy the new machines, and for three years the havoc they committed, especially in Yorkshire, Lancashire, and Nottinghamshire, was immense. It was not until enormous powers were granted to the military, the magistracy, and the police, that the con-

* The notorious " Orders in Council."

spiracy was brought to an end by the execution of thirty of the ringleaders.*

Such was the miserable condition of the labourers, and their meagre powers of combination, at the dawn of the nineteenth century. Everywhere the combination laws were in full force; the truck system was almost universally established, and still further, to make the workman dependent, he was paid at long intervals; and any advances kindly made to him by a generous employer were charged for at the rate of 260 per cent. per annum. Add to these the fact that the men were kept at work sixteen hours out of the twenty-four, and it will be no matter of surprise that they were driven to defy the cruel and unjust laws which oppressed them, and to carry out their object, not only in the most natural of all ways, but by the means with which they were most familiar, namely, by combination.

The progress of industry at last rendered this imperative. The application of steam power to the processes of manufacture, followed by the inventions of Arkwright, Crompton, Hargreaves, at the close of the eighteenth century, and others, had almost annihilated the domestic system of manufacturing. Hitherto weaving had been carried on in private houses

* The "Luddite Rising," as the disaffection has been called, was intensified by the fact that, whereas the operatives were starving, the capitalists were hoarding. Mr. J. R. Green says: "The war enriched the landowner, the capitalist, the manufacturer, the farmer; but it impoverished the poor. It is, indeed, from the fatal years which lie between the Peace of Amiens and Waterloo that we must date that war of classes, that social severance between rich and poor, between employers and employed, which still forms the great difficulty of English politics."

and in sheds adjoining them, as is still the case in some parts of Yorkshire, as, for instance, the villages about Huddersfield and Leeds. Apprentices lived with their masters as part of the family.* It was a common occurrence for the apprentice to marry his master's daughter, and enter into partnership with her father. With the improvement of machinery, however, when several looms were worked by one engine, the domestic system was supplanted by the factory system. The rapid production of new machines ruined the trade of the hand loom weaver. There can be no doubt that the introduction of machinery was *at first* extremely injurious to those whose means of living were affected—as, indeed, every improvement in machinery must injure those who are only able to keep in the old groove. By the invention of machinery the public, who paid less for their goods, and the manufacturers who produced more cloth for the same, or a less outlay, were the gainers. The old weavers were the only losers.†

I have said the men resorted to the means with which they were most familiar, viz. combination. Their experiences on this point have already been sketched, but now a new departure was made. In the beginning of last century the principle of the guilds had extended itself beyond the middle class, and had reached the working classes. More correctly speaking, the capitalists had withdrawn, and left the men to continue and to promote their combination and organization.

---

* In 1806 there were above 100 such apprentices in Armley, a manufacturing village of between 4,000 and 5,000 inhabitants.

† This has always been the case. The objections in 1730 to the "new-fangled machine" (for winnowing) introduced into Scotland are well known.

In 1703 the Watchmakers' Society and the Norman Society were established in London upon the principle of the present friendly societies; and, with others nearly as old, are still in existence. The example thus set was followed by the rapid promotion of similar societies. Such associations, however, were illegal, and their meetings were obliged to be held privately. The "Friendly Society of Iron Founders," which began in 1810, used to meet on dark nights on the peaty wastes and moors on the highlands of the Midland counties, and the archives of the society were buried in the peat. These societies have now ramifications all over the empire, and in England and Wales alone have funds amounting to upwards of £150,000.

It was customary at the beginning of this century for men from various factories to meet at taverns to pay their instalments into the friendly society, the benefit fund, or the burial club. At such gatherings the new state of affairs—as being the subject nearest every workman's heart—naturally became the common topic of conversation. Every phase of the question was thoroughly discussed, and the conduct of the several employers was freely criticized. The operatives naturally inquired why the hardest work and the least pay generally went together. They saw that everything around them was improving except their own condition, and this appeared to be deteriorating. At length some few who worked under a specially severe taskmaster would naturally rebel. They would agree or combine to resist the injustice and oppression under which they suffered. Their friends would not only sympathize with them, but, knowing not how soon they might be placed in a similar position, would help them in their

fight, and thus, what was at first merely a chat over a
glass of beer, soon became a trade union. "Men," says
Mr. W. T. Thornton, "are seldom collected together in
large masses without speedily discovering that union is
strength, and men whose daily avocations obliged them
to be constantly using, and by use to be constantly
sharpening, their wits, were not likely to be backward
in making this discovery."

The origin of the trade unions accounts for a great
many of their peculiar features. As combining was
illegal, the unions disguised themselves as friendly
societies. In framing the rules the founders naturally
looked at such models as they were already possessed
of; and, as wiser men have done, they selected much
that was bad as well as much that was good. It is a
remarkable fact that those rules at present in existence
in trade unions, which give so much offence to employers, are all actual copies of the rules of the ancient
guilds, or reproductions of the provisions of ancient
statutes. The working men invented no absurdities.
It cannot be too often borne in mind that trade unions
are as much a natural development as is the British
Constitution itself, and it is as foolish to expect immediate perfection in the one as finality in the amendments
already effected in the other. The history of the world
teaches us that so universal is frailty that it is not until
every variety of error has been passed through and ex-
hausted that things at last settle into the right course.

The working men, therefore, cannot be blamed for
not discovering that some of the rules they adopted
were hardly consistent with the general progress of
opinion, and it is greatly to their credit that experience
has taught them better. The foolish rules are never

introduced into new societies, and they are being gradually expunged from the rules of the old ones. This must necessarily be a work of time, because several of the old rules have at first sight an appearance of justice, and certainly contain within themselves much that would naturally commend itself to the workmen. Take, for instance, the rules relating to apprentices, in those trades to which no apprenticeship is needed. The rule limiting the number of apprentices is not only characteristic of almost all the guilds and of some of the statutes,* but was copied by the Inns of Court and the Universities, and is, moreover, one that would especially commend itself before the introduction of machinery. In the first place, there was, and is, the desire to limit the number of competitors as much as possible. With a market sufficiently well stocked with workmen, each new arrival would be regarded with great jealousy. Nor is there anything wrong in the notion of restricting the supply of labourers. The point where evil may creep in is found in the means taken to bring about such restrictions. A great authority like Mr. J. S. Mill urged upon the working men the necessity of restricting their numbers as a means of increasing their wages. The plan he recommended was the "prudential check" of Malthus. What, however, seems easy and roseate to the philosopher often appears difficult, if not impracticable, to the ordinary mortal; and the last generation of British workmen took such steps as instantly occurred to them, or were suggested to them, and the results of which were actually before their eyes. Each man would say to himself, "The less number of workers in my trade

* 5 Eliz., c. 4; 5 and 6 Ed. VI., c. 22; 1 James I., c. 6.

the better it is for me." It requires a high state of development to perceive the various and intricate ways in which the laws of production and distribution work so as to bring about the greatest happiness to the greatest number. Another point which would naturally occur to the workman would be that *he* taught the apprentice and received no remuneration. All the trouble and work of training the youth were left to the artisan, and when the pupil was perfect he at once competed with his teacher. During the whole of the seven years' apprenticeship the master received the benefits of the youth's extra labour, and of the premium that was sometimes paid with him, while the man who had borne the heat and burden of the day received no advantage whatever. The rule limiting the number of apprentices, then, was very attractive to the founders of trade unions. The improvements in machinery, however, are rapidly depriving the system of its utility. It may have required a long apprenticeship before a man could weave; it requires little to "mind a loom;" and therefore that rule of the trade unions, which is so often quoted by employers as exhibiting the arbitrary principle of the unions, had a natural birth, is dying a natural death, and will ere long be decently buried and duly forgotten.*

The trade unions copied several other ancient provisions, such as the rules against systematic overtime.

---

* Of course *skilled* trades cannot be learned without a long apprenticeship. Even the Government of this country believes in the advantages of limiting the number of apprentices, as the Board of Trade, in September, 1874, suggested that shipowners should take apprentices according, as to number, to the tonnage of the ship, or, in default, pay a heavy tax.

The guilds also forbade a member to work with a non-member. No member was to instruct another, and " no person of the mystery was to hire himself to a person of another mystery where greater wages were offered." "Rattening" (exactly similar to the Sheffield system, with the exception that in the old times it was legal, and now it is not) was practised against those persons who neglected to pay their subscriptions. The guilds had also their "black lists," and the word "donation," now applied to the money given to men "on tramp," is a translation of "Geo-chenk," the word given by the old German guilds to the workmen who were similarly tramping. These and other rules were copied into the codes of the new unions. They are rapidly becoming obsolete, and are not enforced at all in the iron industries. In these industries no fixed period of service is imposed on apprentices, nor is their number limited. The union men do not refuse to work with non-union men, and "rattening" is not allowed.

From this it is seen that, in the natural order of things, the early trade unionists selected rules which they now ignore. They also showed at times more of the bigotry and narrow-mindedness of a bygone age than one likes to see now. There have been intolerants in every creed, and it would be strange if trade unions had furnished an exception. Even the most partial inquirer would fail to detect any more intolerance in trade unionism than can be found in the society which was presided over by the Duke of Cumberland—or, indeed, in any other combination. It would, however, not have been surprising if intolerance had reached its culminating point in trade unions. The wonder is, not that there has been so much ill-feeling on the part of the men, but that there has been so little. Oppression breeds intolerance. The men knew that it was illegal to combine, and having therefore to conspire, they came to regard both their masters and the laws as their natural enemies, against whom they would have to wage a war prolonged, if not everlasting. "Consciousness," says Thornton, "of being singled out as victims by a partial and iniquitous law, directed exclusively against themselves, naturally excited in them both general prejudice against all law, and special rancour against those in whose behalf the specially obnoxious law had been enacted." Created by strikes, and nurtured by oppression, unions long retained their warlike spirit, a characteristic which now happily is passing away.

It remains to add that combinations began, not amongst the workmen, but amongst the masters. The employed merely followed the example of their employers. It was, and still is, the practice of large capitalists to combine to keep down the price of labour, instead of competing with each other, and so raising wages to their "legitimate rate," as it is called. Until lately the combination of the masters has been directed to a great extent against poor, ignorant, and disunited men, and on that account the capitalists have generally been successful. This state of things is now changed.

It is seen, then, that trade unions were not improvised. They are not sudden and impulsive combinations, carelessly formed to be hastily abandoned. They are the natural outgrowth of natural laws. Workmen soon perceived that all the extra profits arising from improved appliances went into the pockets of the ,

capitalists, and that a great deal of additional misery
and suffering was imposed upon themselves. They
saw that the hardest fare and the most work always
accompanied each other, and there were complaints
loud and deep.   Indeed, trade unions have always
been "forced" into existence by the oppression of the
masters; and when attempts have been made by the
men to establish a union in the absence of pressure
from above they have always failed.*   At this distance
of time we can now clearly see that the employers of
Nottingham must be blamed for the fact that, in 1812,
half the population of their town lived upon public
relief.   To destroy a loom was punishable with death,
and it was then that numerous associations of workmen
sprung into existence.   These associations developed
into trade unions as soon as the law permitted them to
do so.   It can hardly be doubted that the indictment,
fifty-seven yards long, charging some mechanics in 1846
with conspiring to get up a strike, and with some
"thousands" of misdemeanours, was the beginning of
the now large association known as the Amalgamated
Society of Engineers, and if its success was at all
doubtful, the conduct of the Messrs. Platt in 1852
established its basis on a rock.†   It was the violation of

* The first attempt of the London tailors and that of the
puddlers in 1845 are cases in point.

† "After a lock-out of four months, and the expenditure of the
whole of the accumulated funds of the Amalgamated Society, the
employers opened their works again, and the men went back
on the old terms.   Had the Amalgamated Society broken up, as
was confidently expected at the time, the labour movement
might have been thrown back a quarter of a century . . . as it
was, the defeat proved better than a victory.   It was the turning-

13 George IV., cap. 68, by the masters, in favour of
themselves and against the interests of the men, which
led the Spitalfield weavers to form their association.
The oppression of the miners led to the formation of
the union in 1831 ; while the clothworkers, the hatters,
calico printers, the Scotch bakers (who in 1846 were
little better than slaves), and all the new as well as the
old societies, have been forced into existence by the injustice of the employers. " I am no lover of trade
unions," says the Bishop of Manchester, " but they
have been forced upon the working classes by the
inequitable use of the power of capital."

point in the history of the Amalgamated Society, which rapidly
recovered its losses, and at the end of two years was stronger
than ever."—Mr. Thomas Hughes, in *The Century* for May, 1884.

CHAPTER II.

TRADE UNIONS—THEIR PROGRESS AND DEVELOPMENT.

Attempts to crush unionism.—Hornby *v.* Close — Combination
made legal — First conference of union delegates — The
Sheffield outrages—The Royal Commission —Unequal laws
—Picketing—The Trade Union Acts.

THE events whose history has been sketched in the
previous chapter show that combinations amongst workmen have ·existed from a remote period, as well as
indicate the origin of trade unions. It was necessary
thus to trace the historical continuity of the steps that
led to the formation of unions, else their actual objects
would not be clearly defined ; the difficulties encountered
and overcome not sufficiently appreciated ; the basis on
which unions rest not thoroughly understood, and the
future of such institutions not readily realized.

> "We watch the wheels of Nature's mazy plan,
> And learn the future from the past of man."

When, however, the existence of unions became a fact,
their succeeding career was by no means smooth.
Every concession had to be wrung from the legislature by the severest struggles, and there was always
a readiness shown to hamper or destroy them.

The power with which it was thought unionism could
be crushed was very slowly withdrawn. It was not
until 1824 that combinations of working men were
rendered legal for "improving wages and reducing the
hours of labour," and for these two purposes alone.
The statute .which gave this power, however, was anything but satisfactory. The word of the master was
always to be taken in preference to that of the servant;
the judges decided that all combinations which were
"in restraint of trade" were criminal; and the Queen's
Bench in 1867 confirmed the decision of the magistrates
(*vide* Hornby *v.* Close), that societies having rules enabling them so to act could hold no property, not even
for benevolent and charitable purposes. This decision
had reference to boiler-makers and iron shipbuilders,
and created a great sensation. More than one London
newspaper declared a belief and expressed a hope that
by it unionism had received its death blow. The trade
unionists, too, were naturally alarmed; but they were
not prepared to see destroyed an institution which had
been builded up with so much trouble, and in the face
of so many difficulties. A conference of trade union
delegates was convened by the " Working Men's Association," and met in St. Martin's Hall, on March 5, 6,
7, 8, 1867, to consider the matter, as well as the Royal
Commission to inquire into trade unions that the
Government of the day had just appointed.* No such

* The object of the commission was "to inquire into the
organization and rules of trade unions and other associations,
whether of workmen or employers, and into the effect produced
by such unions and associations on the workmen and employers
respectively, and the relations between workmen and employers
and on the trade and industry of the country."

conference had ever been held before. There were present delegates from sixty-five London societies, twelve provincial trade councils, and twenty-five provincial trade societies. This conference was the forerunner of the trade unions congress that is now such a prominent annual public event. The delegates were unanimous in calling for an immediate alteration of the law, and so determined was their aspect that they refused to accept as a compromise the measure introduced into the House of Commons by Mr. Neale, M.P. for Oxford, having for its object a temporary protection to certain of the societies. On the other hand, a resolution was passed, a bill was drafted, and a petition adopted, which I here reproduce. Resolved—

"That, taking into consideration the late decision of the Court of Queen's Bench, in reference to trade unions, depriving them of all legal recognition, and of protection for their funds; further, taking into consideration the benevolent purposes for which the bulk of such funds are subscribed, this meeting of trade delegates is of opinion that it is the bounden duty of the legislature to enact such laws as will protect their funds, and thereby place the members of those societies on the same footing in respect to their funds as all other classes of her Majesty's subjects; and also bearing in mind the fact that the working of these trade unions are to be inquired into by a Royal Commission, and that legislation in respect to them may hereafter take place, we consider that a bill of the following nature will answer that purpose :—

" BILL.

" Whereas combinations or associations of the operative classes for the protection of their trade interests are recognized by law; and whereas it appears that no adequate security is by law provided for the safety of the funds collected by such associations; be it therefore enacted, etc., etc.

" That the same protection shall be given to all members of such combinations or associations of the operative classes in respect to the funds collected for the purposes of the protection of their trade interests as are afforded to the members of Friendly Societies by the Friendly Societies' Act; and shall be recoverable from defaulters in the same way and manner as is provided for in the said Friendly Societies' Act; and that their protection in respect to such funds shall be effectual whether such associations shall be connected with Friendly, Benefit, or Provident Societies, or otherwise, and shall extend to all such funds as are not to be devoted to the promotion of objects criminal in their own nature, but that nothing herein contained shall entitle the office-bearers of such associations or combinations to sue any of their members for arrear of contributions, nor in any respect to coerce any individual to become a member of such association; they shall give any further legal recognition (except as hereinbefore provided for) to such societies as is already given in Law.   This Act to have effect until the end of the Parliamentary session next after the Royal Commission of Inquiry on Trade Unions has given in its report."

The petition was as follows :—

The Humble Petition of the Undersigned Members of the
    Society of   , assembling or meeting at (or in)
         , in the Parish of   , County:

HUMBLY SHEWETH,—

That your Petitioners have seen with deep concern that by the late decision of the Court of Queen's Bench, in the case of Hornby v. Close, this organization of working men, in common with nearly two thousand similar Associations throughout the United Kingdom, are deprived of all legal recognition, and of protection for our funds.

That such funds having been contributed, not merely for what we consider the legitimate protection of our trade interests, but also, and principally, for mutual help and support in seasons of adversity; your Petitioners humbly submit that such a state of the law is an injustice to us as members of the community, will tend to foster fraud and to discourage provident habits; and is, therefore, extremely undesirable to establish or maintain.

Your Petitioners therefore humbly pray your Honourable House forthwith to enact such a law as will give to us, and the members of all such Societies, the same protection for their funds as are enjoyed by all other classes of her Majesty's subjects against fraud and dishonesty.

And your Petitioners will pray, etc.

There were many decisions given, too, by judges and minor magistrates that showed distinctly employers and operatives were not equal when standing before the seat of judgment. The law did not seem particu-

larly just that would not allow men to "picket" in the
tailors' strike, but which allowed the masters to address
a circular to their fellow-employers (being members of
the Master Tailors' Association), asking them not to
employ certain unionist workmen named therein; nor
does that decision (on the same dispute) seem a very
wise one which, acknowledging that the simple act of
one man persuading another is perfectly legal, yet
stated that, because several men organized themselves
to inform workmen that such and such a shop was on
strike, they were deemed guilty of an offence against
the law. Nor could right-minded men be brought to
see the justice of that law which, while it only fined the
master for breach of contract, imprisoned the servant
for the same offence. It was not until 1871 that an
Act was passed remedying these defects. The law on the
subject even then was, unfortunately, very ambiguous
and imperfect. The unjust, cruel, and blundering imprisonment of the gas stokers showed that there was
still plenty of scope for cunning lawyers when pleading
to an excited jury and before a prejudiced judge. As a
matter of fact the whole tendency of legislation for the
men by the masters has ever been to keep wages low.
Indeed, that has been the avowed object of the laws
which have been passed. To counteract this, the
unions were formed to keep them high, and we have
the authority of a man who believed in a high moral
standard that such conduct was praiseworthy. "If it
were possible," wrote Mr. J. S. Mill, "for the working
classes, by combining among themselves, to raise or
keep up the general rate of wages, it need hardly be
said that this would be a thing not to be punished, but
to be welcomed and rejoiced at." The further im-

provements in the law in this respect will be noticed in
due course.

At this time trade unions were regarded unfavour-
ably by a large portion of the public in consequence of
what was known as the Sheffield outrages. "In order
to compel men to join their unions and comply with the
rules, a system had been adopted of taking away the
tools and driving bands of independent or defaulting
workmen, and this system had become so universal that
when tools or bands had been stolen, the sufferers
applied systematically to the secretary of the union to
know on what terms the lost articles would be restored.
But the unionists were not long content with this
exercise of their power, and proceeded to the execution
of a series of outrages and crimes which are perhaps
almost without parallel in the history of communities
supposed to be civilized. Masters and workmen who
refused or failed to comply with their rules, were subjected to treatment of the most diabolical character.
Their cattle were hamstrung, or otherwise mutilated,
their ricks set on fire. They were shot at, and in one
instance a master was killed by an air gun fired into a
crowded room. Gunpowder was usually employed in
the case of obnoxious workmen. Canisters were thrown
down chimneys, bottles filled with the explosive, to which
lighted fusees were attached, were thrown through
windows of the workmen's dwelling-houses, thus exposing women and children to its terrible effects. It
was a common practice to place gunpowder in grinding
troughs, which exploded as soon as work was commenced." * In justice to the great body of workmen at
Sheffield, it should be stated that these outrages were

* "Trade Unionism." By Mr. William Saunders.

committed by a very few persons, and were at all times execrated by the great body of the working classes. Out of sixty trade unions, then in existence, twelve were implicated in these outrages, and of these it was shown on inquiry that the greater proportion of the members knew nothing of the actions of their officers.

The result of the Sheffield outrages was, that a Royal Commission was appointed in 1867 to inquire into the matter and into the condition of trade unions generally. The conference of delegates already alluded to urged upon the Government that a trade unionist representative should sit upon the commission. The request was refused, but ultimately a concession was made that Mr. Frederic Harrison, barrister-at-law, a well-known advocate of unionism and possessing the confidence of the unionists, should sit on the commission, and he rendered signal services in that position. The trade unionists also asked to be present at the inquiry to " watch " their interests. This also was refused, but the point was immaterial as the House of Lords amended the constitution of the commission by throwing its doors open to the press and the public. The disclosures before the commission are now a matter of history. The authors of the outrages were discovered only on their own confession, made under a promise of pardon, and thus they escaped punishment.

The good points of trade unions were also fully placed before the commission by the best of the unions' secretaries, whose evidence will well repay perusal at this day. Altogether the inquiry raised trade unions in the estimation of the public. It was seen that, purged of their impurities, they would be excellent institutions, and the legislature set to work to give

them a legal status.   In 1871 the Trade Union Act
was passed, making trade unions legal societies, and
preventing the members from being liable to prosecution
for conspiracy, an offence for which, in days gone by,
so many had suffered imprisonment ; while by an inter-
pretation given to Russell Gurney's Act of 1868, due
protection was given to the funds of the society.   In
short, trade unions were now acknowledged to be institutions of the country.   They had henceforth a charter
of liberty, and under the light and freedom so given to
them they began to flourish, and, as will be shown in the
succeeding pages, have continued to flourish, to the welfare of the working classes, and the general benefit of
the whole commonwealth.

CHAPTER III.

TRADE UNIONS—THEIR OBJECTS.

Equality of bargaining power—To raise wages—Protection—Sick
  benefits, etc.—Mutual support—Moral improvement of the
  workman — Constitution of a union — The Amalgamated
  Society of Engineers—Executive of unions prevents strikes
  —Unselfishness of unionism—Trade unions congresses—
  Their influence—The International—The Paris conference—
  Trade councils in New Zealand.

THE foregoing account of the origin of trade unions is
almost an answer to the question, "What are the
objects of trade unions?" The question must at all
times be difficult to answer in a sentence, because the
scope of the objects of unionism grows with the growth
of unionism. At first they were merely a protection
against contracts being *too* unjust, too heavy to be
borne. They now demand—and rightly so—that contracts shall be fair. Mr. Dunning says the object of a
trade union is "to ensure the freedom of exchange with
regard to labour, by putting the workman on something
like an equal position in bargaining with his employer."
Professor Fawcett takes a similar view. Trade unions
are formed, he says, so "that the labourer may have
the same chance of selling his labour dearly as the
master has of buying it cheaply." At a later date,

the same authority declares the intention of the men to have been " to protect themselves against what are supposed to be the conflicting interests of their employers." So, too, Mr. Frederic Harrison believes that, at any rate, "the all-important question is how equality is to be established," and he represents the placing of labour on the same footing as capital as the great *desideratum.* Mr. W. T. Thornton, however, admits of no such object as the abstract idea of equality. The object of unionism, he maintains, is not merely to free men from the dictation of their employers, but to change positions, and to dictate; and that "their rule is to get as much as they can, and to keep as much as they can get." "The single aim of trade unions," he says, "is to enable themselves to dictate arbitrarily the conditions of employment." Mr. Joseph Gostrick takes an opposite view. "The main object," he writes, " of all the best and most intelligent members of English trade unions is not to obtain the highest possible rate of wages, but to render the working man's employment and his means of subsistence *less precarious.*" (The italics are his own.)

Although the evidence given before the Trade Union Commission by some of the most intelligent and trustworthy of the trade union secretaries endorses such views as those expressed by Mr. Thornton, yet the history of the movement shows that although unions may have been founded principally, if not solely, as protective associations, and have developed to some extent into aggressive associations, yet they have long ago embraced other features in their objects. They now aim at every means that will raise workmen to the best position it is possible for them to obtain. The

United Joiners of Glasgow describe the objects of their society as "the protection and elevation of the members of such institutions, and the amelioration of the working class in general." Among other objects the Amalgated Society of Joiners and Carpenters, as well as other societies, includes the raising of funds for "The mutual support of its members in case of sickness, accident, superannuation, for the burial of members and their wives, emigration, loss of tools by fire, water, or theft, and for assistance to members out of work." The late Mr. Alex. Macdonald, M.P., thinks it is quite within the province of a trade union to press upon Parliament the necessity of "securing provisions for the health of the miner while at his work below ground," as well as to urge for measures to "prevent explosions," if not even to look after the proper distribution of funds voluntarily subscribed for the relief of sufferers from calamities. Under the auspices of the Amalgamated Carpenters and Joiners industrial schools have been promoted for the furtherance of technical education. Other societies lay great stress upon lectures, while others again show great anxiety as to the morals of their members. In the lodges of the London bricklayers swearing and drunkenness are not allowed, and the London Compositors' Society has a circulating library, while the Birkenhead Trades Council conducted an agitation for public baths. A most welcome sign of the times is the application, a few weeks ago, by the Northumberland and Durham Miners' Union for the extension of university teaching in their district. This is the first request of the kind made by a trade union, and, taken with the establishment of the farthing scheme for the Welsh college, indicates that workmen are alive to the advantages of high-class education, and are determined to avail themselves fully of such opportunities.

An impartial inquirer, then, will take a higher view of the object of trade unionism than Mr. Thornton believes in without being liable to a charge of sentimentalism. The object of a trade union is a wide one, viz., to do all that can be done to better in every respect the condition of its members. The raising of the rate of wages is undoubtedly the principal means to that end, but to say that it is the "sole aim" is to mistake the one for the other. Based upon union, the efforts of these organizations are collective, and the results general, not special. Unlike most kinds of individual effort, the object is not to assist men to lift themselves out of their class, as if they were ashamed of it, or as if manual labour were a disgrace, but to raise the class itself in physical well-being and self-estimation.

No encyclopædia has yet devoted an article to trade unions, and yet trade unionism is an accomplished fact. They are built on a rock—a firm, sound, substantial basis. They cannot be annihilated. If they were done away with to-day, they would spring up again to-morrow, the same as in the celebrated dispute with Messrs. Platt, of Oldham; when the men were starved into submission and were obliged to give up their union, yet they rejoined as soon as they were at work. Although unionism in Lancashire languished during the cotton famine, it sprang into life with renewed vigour when the crisis was over. It would be well if the employers at present (March, 1884) endeavouring to crush out unionism amongst the engineers of

Sunderland would take warning from these facts. It
is a mistake to say that unions are the cause of hostility between labour and capital; they are the result
of that hostility. It will be well for the masters to
remember this. It will be well for them to realize the
fact that unions will not decrease in power as some
persons fondly hope. Wherever there has been intelligence there has been combination. Professor Fawcett
pointed out in 1871 that there was no combination
amongst the agricultural labourers because they were
"too ignorant," and because there was a "want of
intelligence." They quietly submitted in North Here-
fordshire to a pittance of nine or ten shillings a week,
whilst their fellow-labourers in Warwickshire were
getting twelve shillings a week, and probably they
were so inured to suffering that they would never have
complained had they not been persistently subjected
to pitiless, relentless, and objectless cruelty. It is a
fact that the most intelligent of our artisans are the
most earnest advocates of trade unions, and these have
not been slow to instruct their less fortunate brethren
of the advantages of unionism; and although the way
in which the last great agricultural dispute ended may
not be satisfactory, still the union is established, and
will yet accomplish its end. The power of trade unions
will increase with experience, and their influence will
extend as education becomes general. It is for the
masters to say whether they will bow to a necessity
graciously, or, as hitherto, goad to the last extremity.
Day by day the men are becoming less and less
dependent upon the caprice of the masters. Their
demand for just laws cannot longer be disregarded, and
even now they are able to show that they are as com-

petent as any other class to take care of their own
personal habits and requirements.

The unions, formed in the manner described, spread
rapidly. They did not long confine themselves to the
villages or towns in which they began, but the "unions"
in various places "amalgamated," and thus influenced
large areas. They extended their ramifications still
wider, and they embraced the whole kingdom, and even
obtained a footing in America and Australia.

The constitution of a union, then, will be easily
imagined; but it may not be amiss, nevertheless, if a
few words are devoted to a description of one as a
model. Let that one be the Amalgamated Society of
Engineers. According to the thirty-third annual
report of that society, it appears that in 1883 the union
consisted of 424 branches, chiefly in towns in the
British Isles, but with a fair sprinkling in Canada, the
United States, Australia, India, and other parts of
the globe. The number of members was 50,418. A
branch must consist of not less than seven members,
nor more than 300. The constitution is pre-eminently democratic. Each branch is itself a completely
organized body. It selects and elects its own officers;
it collects, holds, and spends its own funds; and it
manages the whole of the business which affects itself
alone. The officers of the branch are elected at general
meetings, at which every member must be present,
under the penalty of a fine. Members who refuse to
be nominated for office, or who refuse to serve if
elected, are also subject to fines; and officers who
neglect their business, either by coming late to meetings or absenting themselves altogether, are similarly
punished. A meeting of the members of each branch

is held every fortnight for the transaction of ordinary
business, such as receiving subscriptions and deciding
upon propositions for new members. These meetings
begin at half-past seven in the evening and close at
half-past nine or ten o'clock, but the hours are altered
when it is found that it is more convenient to do so.
The duties of the secretary are onerous, and his responsibility is great. No one, therefore, is eligible who has
not been in the society two years successively, and " no
member shall be elected as secretary who keeps a public
or beer house." He has to keep the accounts of his
branch and conduct its correspondence. He has to see
to the payment of members who are entitled to travelling relief, donation, sick, superannuation, or funeral
benefit. He has to summon meetings, keep minutes,
report to the general secretary as to the state of the
trade of the district, the number of men out of work ,
and the branch of their trade; or, on the other hand,
he has to state if men are wanted, and if so, in what
departments; and he has also " to transact any other
business that belongs to his office." There are pre-
cautions also surrounding this and the other officers.
The president, vice-president, and assistant secretary
of a branch are elected quarterly; and if a man be
10s. in arrears with his contributions he cannot take
office. Members are also exempt if they be upwards
of fifty years of age, or if they reside more than three
miles from the club-house. Any complaint as to the
way in which the officers do their work must be sent to
a referee, who, like the secretary, is elected annually.
The referee must place the matter before a branch
meeting, and if he himself neglects any of his duties
he is fined half a crown. There are also book-keepers,

E

money stewards, doorkeepers, treasurers, and auditors, the nature of whose work is evident from their titles. There are also sick-stewards, whose duties are to visit the sick "twice a week," to report their visits to the meetings of the branch, and to carry the invalid his "sick benefit." None of the offices are honorary. In branches numbering less than 50 members every officer is allowed 4*d*., and in branches numbering 50 and upwards 6*d*., for his attendance on branch meeting nights. The secretary is paid annually, and according to the size of the branch. The lowest amount is £1 5*s*. for a branch of 10 members; the highest £10 4*s*., for a branch of 300. The auditors are paid at a lower rate, which varies from 9*d*. to 4*s*. 8*d*., while the treasurer is paid 10 per cent. on the sum set apart for use.

Each branch has also a committee, which has power to determine anything whereon the society's rules are silent. The books of the branch are open to their inspection; they can summon meetings, and they have various other duties. Each member of this committee receives 6*d*. for each meeting he attends, and is fined 6*d*. for each meeting from which he is absent.

In any district where there are more branches than one, a local district committee must be formed, consisting of seven members, each branch, as nearly as practicable, selecting an equal number. Where there are seven branches each one sends a representative. The duties of this committee are to "watch over the interests of the trade, and transact such business as affects the district generally." It must not, however, interfere with the business appertaining to any particular branch of the society. It would be superfluous to more minutely discuss the constitution of this committee. Its election, payment, fining, etc., of officers are identical in principle, though different in detail, to the same things in the branches.

Here, then, we have first the individual; second, the branch, with its committee, formed of an association of individuals;* third, a district committee, formed indirectly of an association of branches; and when it is thought desirable this principle is extended, in the shape of a central district committee. The fountain head, however, is not yet reached. The central authority is vested in a general or executive council, consisting of 37 members, of whom 11 represent metropolitan branches, the others being from the provinces, including Scotland and Ireland. To sit on this council is a high honour, and candidates for the position must have been members of the society for five years. As the country councillors cannot conveniently attend frequent meetings in London, the ordinary management is entrusted to the 11 London members (who are called the local council), and the council is also further broken up into various committees for managing the details of the society. This council hears appeals from branches, advises, forbids, initiates, and terminates strikes. The general secretary receives a salary of £4 per week, and lives rent free. He also receives 1s. 6d. each time he attends a council meeting, and is paid for any special journeys undertaken or extra work done. His assistants receive £2 10s. a week, and have to give the

---

* Some societies, as, for instance, those of the compositors, have an intervening institution, formed by the men employed in certain establishments, the duty of which is to see that engagements are faithfully carried out.

whole of their time to the association. They have to compile and issue a monthly report, as well as quarterly and yearly reports. The last-named is quite a formidable volume, consisting of nearly 400 pages of large post octavo, and those of other societies are like unto it. His hours of business are fixed at from nine a.m. to six p.m. He has power to authorize members that are on donation to be removed from one branch to another where there is a probability of employment, and he has to keep a register of all the members of the society, stating when and where admitted or re-admitted, age, married or not, and whether a member has received any part of the financial money. Mr. Macdonald, in his evidence before the Trade Union Commission, summed up his duties as a trade union secretary by observing that in seven years he had attended 1600 meetings, travelled 230,000 miles, and written 17,000 letters. It remains to add, that above the council there is the right of appeal to a meeting of delegates from all the branches, and in some instances there can be a direct appeal to the members of the society, who, indeed, frequently elect the secretary.

No trade union is subsidized. The funds arise from the contributions of members. In the Amalgamated Society of Engineers the contribution generally is one shilling a week, and if a man be in arrears he is suspended from the benefits of the society—unless, indeed, he is out of work, or in distressed circumstances. According to the last report of our model association, the number of members had increased in 1883 to 50,418, and they had a balance in hand of £178,125, or upwards of £3 10s. a man.

Such is a rough outline of the nature of a trade

union. Others are like unto it, though it must be observed that the federal principle is not universal. Some unions possess a more centralized system, the chief officer having entire control of the funds and of everything else. The National Agricultural Labourers' Union is a case in point, in contradistinction to the Federal Union of Agricultural Labourers; and feeling on the difference of constitution was carried so far that the agents of the former refused to co-operate with those of the latter in order to bring the dispute to an end.* The federal principle, however, is the one most in favour, and indeed seems to be the one most just and natural. The recent and disastrous dispute in the cotton trade, already alluded to, appears to have taught the operatives this salutary lesson. The disjointed and powerless associations that, without ample funds, struck in the face of a falling market, despite the warnings of their leaders, have now formed themselves into the "Amalgamation of the Northern Counties Association;" and the first action of the new amalgamation has been to secure, without any strike, the restoration of the five per cent. reduction of February last.

No sketch of a trade union can give any idea of the scrupulous care that is taken to do that which is lawful and right. The code of rules of a trade union bristles with judicious safeguards. The ideas that a strike depends upon the *ipse dixit* of a paid agitator, and that if the men were to vote by ballot on the question, they

---

Mr. Joseph Arch writes to the author: "Our Union is based on centralization so far as funds and management are concerned; but every officer is elected by the popular vote. I don't think we should have held our own as we have had we not centralized our force."

would never consent to a strike, are conceived by those only who do not know what a trade union is. In most cases a strike is the result of action taken by the men themselves in each district, the executive having more power to prevent a strike than to initiate one. So recently as the last cotton strike (1883–4) the executive did all they could to prevent the strike, but the operatives rushed into it in spite of the protestations of all the leaders. It must have surprised some people a few years ago to read that the members of the Hand Mule Spinners' Association not only vote by ballot, but that there must be a majority of two-thirds in favour of a strike before one can be declared; and yet when the dispute in September, 1874, at Bolton was decided upon, the numbers were—For a strike, 1034; against, 77. Nor must it be thought that when polled the men vote rashly. They do not, as a rule, vote in favour of a strike unless they think not only that they have right on their side, but that they will be able to establish that right. From a report of the Amalgamated Boot and Shoe Makers' Association we learn that the result of a poll was as follows :—*

That the advance movement does proceed this summer ... 917
That the advance movement does *not* proceed until we have
   sufficient funds to meet the expenses 2315

And again—

That the contributions be raised one halfpenny {For ... 2291
  per week ... ... {Against 472

As a proof of the care taken to avoid strikes, may be mentioned that several of the most powerful unions in the kingdom have made a rule that in no case shall aid

* See also page 104.

be given to any local branch, unless it can be proved that before going out a *bonâ fide* offer of arbitration has been made to the employer. The secretaries, or executive, too, always warn their union to avoid causes of dispute. Quite recently, Mr. E. Woods, the able secretary of the Ironfounders' Society, warned its members that "the general outlook evidently points to the unpleasant conclusion that business is on the decline." That being so, it was counselled that the "inevitable" should be prepared for not only by husbanding resources, but by avoiding causes of disputes. Facts, too, are stubborn things. "It was confidently expected," says Mr. Thos. Hughes in the *Century*, "that strikes would grow in numbers and intensity as the unions spread over larger areas;" but "of late years the number of these strikes has notably diminished; and every year the chances of such lamentable contests seem likely to decrease." It should be noted further, that Mr. Frederic Harrison, at the last Trade Union Congress, and Mr. George Howell, in the *Contemporary Review*, pointed out that "last year (1882) the Amalgamated Engineers, with an income of £124,000, and a cash balance of £168,000, expended in disputes altogether, including the support they gave to other trades, the sum of £895 only. That was far less than one per cent. of their income. The Ironfounders spent out of an income of £42,000, £214 only; and the Amalgamated Carpenters, who had had a number of disputes and had been engaged in strikes, spent £2000 only out of £50,000, which was only four per cent.; the Tailors, with £18,000, spent £565 only; and the Stonemasons, with 11,000 members in union—the report seems to say more in sorrow than pride—spent nothing in strikes. During six years of unexampled bad trade, reduction of wages, and industrial disturbance, there were a great many strikes, and during that period seven great trade societies expended in the settlement of disputes £162,000 only out of a capital of nearly £2,000,000. Last year these societies, with an aggregate income of £330,000, and a cash balance of £360,000, expended altogether in matters of dispute about £5000, which was not two per cent. upon the whole of their income, and not one per cent. upon their total available resources for the year." The rules of unions, too, are so framed that the work of the officers of the union is not interfered with by the duties of their office. Thus no member must call on an officer when he is at his ordinary work under a penalty of one shilling; and there are many wise and prudent regulations, the most important of which will be pointed out in due course.

A remarkable feature in trade unionism is its thorough unselfishness. The various societies are not opposed to each other; indeed, they help one another. Every assistance is given to those who are prepared to sacrifice whatever benefits are to be derived from living in this country by emigrating to another. Working men realize the fact that by *some* going *all* are benefited. Not only do they cheerfully submit to the ordinary contributions of an entrance fee and a weekly subscription, but they are ever ready to pay an extra levy, sometimes for their own trade purposes, but very often for ulterior objects, such as assisting Mr. Plimsoll in his agitation. The noble way in which almost every union helped the agricultural labourers, and in which some of them subscribed to the relief fund for the famine in India, will not easily be forgotten. This sacrifice by the indi-

vidual for the benefit of the community contrasts
favourably with the thoroughly selfish programme of
the National Federation of Associated Employers of
Labour, and probably accounts for the general tendency
to victory on the side of the men whenever disputes
arise. The masters do not try to help each other.
They are in opposition to each other. Their motto is
"Each for himself," and they are only united in their
attempts to crush the men. The men, on the other
hand, it is worth repeating, sink all individual feelings,
and help each other in a thoroughly practical and
praiseworthy manner.

It remains to point out that the principle of unionism
is extending beyond individual trades. In all large
towns there are trade councils, formed of delegates
from various unions. These councils look after the
general interests of the unionists in the area represented, and an attentive reader of the public prints
cannot have failed to notice that they are as ready to
censure the action of union members who have done
wrong as to support the action of those who are in the
right. The growth of unionism shows itself still further
in the annual congress which is now held. This is a
thoroughly national institution, and its arrangements
allow of the widest possible latitude in the subjects for
discussion. It is now sixteen years since the "Labour
Parliament" began (at Manchester) its annual sittings,
and if there were no other evidence of the great good
unionism accomplishes, the work of the Trade Unions
Congress would be ample testimony. Many most beneficent acts of Parliament are directly due to the action
of the congress, and others have been, and others again
are being, improved by the same influence. The Em-

ployers' Liability Bill is a case in point, and testifies also to the persistent industry and ability with which all obstacles are removed and all difficulties overcome. The extension of the Factory Acts to workshops is another instance, as is also the Act for the better Regulation of Mines; while the protection afforded to wages by alterations in the Bankrupt Law is also due to the direct influence of the parliamentary committee of the congress. At present it is exerting its powers to have a proper inspection of boilers; a proof of the competency of engine drivers; the protection of merchant seamen, and a great many other things. In addition, the congress, as has been said, exerts its influence on many questions that may not at first sight appear really "labour questions." While disavowing party politics, it urges that workmen should be enfranchised; that the Corrupt Practices Act should cheapen the cost of elections so that labour may have a chance of direct representation in Parliament; that alterations in the criminal law shall not affect workmen differently to other people; and that artisans shall be jurymen, factory inspectors, and otherwise act on those occasions wherein the artisan and the operative are as much concerned as anybody else. Added to which it should be observed that the annual gathering together of the picked unionists of the country must tend to strengthen the feeling of brotherhood amongst them which is the basis on which unionism rests.*

* When the Trade Union Congress first started, it was made the medium of addresses in favour of the principles of unionism by gentlemen of position, not members of any union. It was soon seen that these addresses, however interesting, were not of that practical business character for which the congress met, and were

It is easy to see whitherward this tendency points. From a national congress to an international congress is a very short step. The Trade Union Congress of 1879 passed a resolution in favour of a federation of all the trades of the United Kingdom, and thorough unionists desire to see a federation of all the trades throughout the world. An international congress was successfully attempted some years ago, and failed at last only because of the socialism so characteristic of the continental *ouvrier*, who dreams of an exterminating war against a class, instead of seeking to do that which the International Society originally intended to do, viz., to make trade unionism cosmopolitan instead of national.

delivered to a body of men who obviously required no proof of the principles they held; and the practice was at length forbidden by a standing order "that papers in defence of trade unions are unnecessary." Facilities, however, are always given for addresses on general subjects affecting labour, by competent authorities, at times which do not interfere with the business of the congress. Another and an important point that was found to require altera-tion was that in the early days of the congress the regulations for the admission of delegates were not sufficiently stringent, or, more correctly speaking, were not carried out with proper rigour. A peculiar circumstance brought the matter to a crisis. The paid agitators of a "Fair Trade" organization had offered their services as delegates gratuitously to certain unions, and these, actuated by a false economy, accepted those services. The agitators presented themselves for admission at the congress of 1881 (held in London), but after some discussion were expelled—the rule that delegates should be formally elected, and their expenses paid by the society which sent them being on this occasion carried out, despite pre-cedent; and the matter was finally set at rest by a resolution "that no one should be eligible as a delegate whose expenses are paid by private individuals, or by any institutions not *bonâ fide* trade unions or trade councils."

The experience of the late International Association will enable the promoters of a new one, inevitable sooner or later, to arrange matters upon as sound a basis as are trade unions in this country. The leading trade unionists in England realize the fact, and are not afraid to express it. The germ of the organization is present in the foreign branches of some of the largest unions, and it is no uncommon thing for the working men here to assist their brethren in disputes abroad. To almost all the meetings of the Trade Unions Congress come messages from their continental friends. In 1878 it was from the "International Labour Union," in 1879 it was from the Trade Unions of Germany. In 1881 the workmen of Switzerland similarly approached their English friends; and last year (1883) came an invitation from Paris that was cordially accepted. The friendly feeling towards each other of workmen in different countries, and the international relationships that are springing up, were illustrated in 1874 and in 1882 by the visit to England of deputations from the railway servants of France and Belgium; and still more recently by the reciprocal visits of the London and Paris cabmen. The secretary of the Amalgamated Carpenters and Joiners, in one of his reports, says:— "It is gratifying to know that ample funds are at our disposal whenever they may be required, and that our British members will gladly assist their American brethren in their hour of need, knowing that whenever they, in their turn, may labour under similar difficulties, our American members will feel a pride and a pleasure in doing all they can to show that, although separated by the broad Atlantic, we are united by kindred interest and cordial sympathies, having one object in view—the

common good of all. I trust that in this hour of
adversity our fellow-workmen in America will learn
the true value of a great 'International Trade Organization," conducted on equitable and sound financial
principles, having one common fund, available whenever
its members may require assistance. If the industrial
classes in Europe and America fully realized the advantages to be attained by unity of action, their interests
would become so interwoven that wars would become
impossible, and no political jealousies would be permitted to endanger the lives of peaceable citizens, or to
disturb the commercial intercourse which is essential
to the well-being of the people." This noble sentiment
is peculiar to workmen. The employers have not yet
learned to love one another. It is a sentiment, however,
that is rapidly spreading, and in high quarters. Professor Thorold Rogers, in his admirable work so often
quoted, says, "I confess that I look forward to the
international union of labour partnerships as the best
prospect the world has of coercing those hateful in-
stincts of governments, all alike irresponsible and in-
different, by which nations are perpetually armed
against each other, to the infinite detriment, loss, and
demoralization of all."

In response to the invitation of last year, just referred to, the Trade Unions Congress empowered Mr.
E. W. Bailey, Mr. John Burnett, and Mr. Henry Broadhurst and others to attend the conference in Paris of
representative working men of France, Italy, and Spain,
and I will allow those gentlemen to express their views
on the matter in their own words by giving a conden-
sation of their official report. "The conference was
presided over by Messrs. Broadhurst and Shipton and by

Miss Simcox, and by the French, Italian, and Spanish delegates successively. Mr. Burnett presided over the first public meeting, and Mrs. Heatherley over the third. The French procedure in business is different from our own. They discuss a question generally. They attempt to form a resolution to meet the expression of opinion given in debate. So far as our experience went, this mode is not so expeditious as the custom adopted by us, of drawing up a resolution and debating it, and then amending it as may be found necessary. We found that the chief work lay in the debate in committee over the terms of the resolutions. At one time it looked as though the conference would fail in this work; however, this undesirable event was avoided, and our subsequent business became more agreeable and easy. The point of difference was the extent to which the State should be asked to protect labour.

"Our time was too much occupied with meetings to admit of much investigation into the number, the extent, and strength of the Paris trade unions; but so far as we could gather, it appeared that the compositors, the engineers, the smiths, and the carpenters possessed the best unions. Even these cannot be compared with the British unions in stability or discipline. The difficulty appears to be to get them to pay contributions of more than twopence a week. Even this sum is only paid by a comparatively small number of the men. The masons' delegate stated that out of some thousands of masons who accepted the principles of their society, only about sixty men were regular subscribers. From this statement, and from other things which came under our observation, it would appear that the numerical strength of an association is reckoned upon the basis of the number of those in the given trade who approve of the objects of the union, and not upon the number of those who contribute to the funds, such as they are. It was upon this loose condition of things that the English delegates made their strongest attack, by stating the condition of membership in Great Britain, and appealed to the members to exert themselves in making the societies more solid and numerous.

" From what came under our notice, we are of opinion that the condition of the workpeople (*i.e.*, the mechanics) in Paris is not so good as that of corresponding trades in Great Britain. We met an English mason in Paris, who is engaged, by an English firm of contractors, at the erection of a Protestant church. He informed us that he was receiving London wages (viz., ninepence an hour), out of which he paid eighteen francs a week (15*s.*) for a furnished room, firing, and the use of a kitchen, the latter shared amongst three families. A shoemaker, who was a delegate at the conference, said that men in his trade were working fourteen hours a day for three and a half francs (2*s.* 11*d.*). These and similar statements made by other delegates, in reference to some of the provinces of France, would seem to prove that the condition of other French workpeople in the large centres and at large works is anything but an enviable one.

" With the exception of a wish to rely upon the State for things they may do for themselves, we did not object to the general views of the French delegates on social questions. A delegate from the carpenters (M. Tortellier) was an exception. He was in favour of revolution by force, but we were informed that this person was under a sentence of imprisonment, and would serve his term of punishment at his convenience. The natural inference to be drawn from this statement was that he was, in the interest of the reactionary party, doing his best to cause strife ; thus affording a pretext for the continuance of the French law relating to labour combinations, which we have no hesitation in saying is a disgrace to, and an anomaly in, a Republican nation.

"The speeches of the French delegates contained constant reference to, and condemnation of, the *bourgeois*, *i.e.*, the middle classes. It would appear that there is little or no intercourse between the workmen and the middle classes in France, and the former, therefore, look upon the latter as their natural enemies; but we are bound to say that the want of intimacy is not only obvious in the cases referred to, but it is also true, to a lamentable extent, between the various groups of workmen themselves. We are painfully alive to the differences between workmen in our own country, and to its deterrent effect upon our thought and progress, but, happily, it does not exist here to such a degree as it does in France.

"We have here given a *résumé* of our delegation. We do not now offer any definite opinions as to the ultimate issue of the conference in relation to the future intercourse between the peoples of the United Kingdom and the peoples of the continental nations. We hope it may bear some fruit. We are assured of one thing, and that is that the British trade unions have not suffered by the contact with their foreign associates. We should be open to the charge of vanity if we ventured to hope that our continental brethren had benefited by our intercourse with them."

As a proof of the tendency to international combination, I may state that at the moment of going to press I have received a copy of communications from the Trade and Labour Council of Otago and Auckland, which communications have been sent to all the trade unions in Great Britain. They are to the effect "that the labour market of New Zealand is largely over-stocked. The present immigration policy of the Government is mainly the cause of it. From all the large centres of population we are constantly hearing of the large number of unemployed. To counteract this evil it has been decided by the above council that the accompanying resolution shall be printed and largely circulated throughout the United Kingdom through the medium of the various trade associations, and also by publishing the same in the leading journals at home. The council feel it is only doing its duty, and carrying out one of the objects for which it was formed, namely, the general welfare of the working classes. The council, along with other organizations of a similar character, feel that the working man's side of all questions is too often overlooked, and that every legitimate means must be taken to counteract the large interests that are at work against them." The following is the resolution referred to:—" That in the present depressed state of the labour market in New Zealand, consequent to a large extent on the present immigration policy being carried out by the Government, this council is unanimously of opinion that the further introduction of all classes of labour is detrimental to the interests of the wages-earning classes, both here and at home." In Antwerp, Ghent, and Brussels, too, the cabinet-makers have recently been holding meetings, and have decided to form a union on

F

the plan of the Alliance Cabinet-makers' Association of England; and indeed, any one who reads the official documents of the trade unions of the United Kingdom cannot but be struck with the close intercourse with the workmen of other nations, with a view that no person taking work in a foreign country shall undersell the workmen of that country.

It is seen, then, that a trade union is pre-eminently fitted for the work it has to do, as must necessarily be the case when the work to be done has created the organization, and not that the organization has created the work to be done. The power to take men whence they are not wanted, and to carry them—abroad if necessary—where there is work to do; the care that is taken of the interests of the men, as opposed to the aggression of the master, as shown by the frequent reports of the branch secretaries on the trade of their districts; the ability to support men "on strike;" the way in which the unions assist each other, and the ease with which additional contributions are successfully levied;* and the fund that is reserved for sickness, emigration, accidents, superannuation, burials, etc.— of which more hereafter—are all evidences of the willingness of the men to obey an organization in which they have confidence, and which they believe is working for their good.

* This was forcibly illustrated during the recent severe depression of trade. See Mr. Geo. Howell's article in the *Contemporary Review* for September, 1883.

CHAPTER IV.

TRADE UNIONS—THEIR EFFICACY.

They have raised wages — Proofs and instances — How much
have the unions raised wages? — The unions a record
of the state of the labour market—Wages would not rise
quickly but for unions—"An unsuccessful strike often succeeds"—Local strikes affect distant areas and many trades
—The agricultural labourers—Where unionism is weak, wages
are low—Shorter hours, yet more work—Piece-work—Errors
of unions—Difficulties of the union secretary—Foolish strikes
injurious, may prevent a rise of wages—A fair day's wages—
Employers' combinations — Boards of arbitration — Trade
unions prevent strikes—Spread of unionism—The power of
trade unions acknowledged by the employers—Trade unions
as friendly and benefit societies—Women's trade unions—
Other features of trade unions, some obsolete—Proceedings
of unions should be public.

ALTHOUGH, as has been shown in the preceding chapter,
the very nature of a well-organized trade union shows
its fitness for the work it has to do, yet it will be
satisfactory if it can be shown that they do their work
well. The question then arises—Have they been successful? Do they carry out the objects for which they
are formed?

Let us ask, in the first place, "Have they succeeded
in raising wages in the past?"

It seems so natural that combination should raise wages, that one is amazed such a position can be questioned. As things at present are, the relations between employers and employed imply a pecuniary bargain. Can it be doubted that when workmen combine they are much more likely to adjust the bargain on more favourable terms to themselves than if they had no power of organized action? Those even who are unwilling to admit the efficacy of trade unions cannot help showing at times—unconsciously, perhaps—that they have an opposite conviction; and some time ago one who is least friendly to trade organizations pointed out that the secret of the attachment of the Southern States of America to slave labour "lay chiefly in the obtaining labour at will at a rate which cannot be controlled by any combination."

Now, in looking over the history of trade unions, no impartial observer can doubt for one moment that the masters have been gradually giving way. In 1845 Mr. W. T. Thornton had already called attention to the fact that the result of trade unions had been to raise wages. In the baking trade in Edinburgh and Glasgow, and other Scotch towns, before 1846, the men were little better than vassals. They lived with their employers, in cheerless celibacy; they were locked in their rooms at nine o'clock at nights; and, in short, being driven by oppression into union, they raised wages 20 per cent., improved their condition, and are now a sober and steady class of men. In 1873 the General Alliance of Operative House Painters asked for higher wages, and the answer was an increase in the rate of pay amounting to £8000 a year. The annual report for 1873 of the Amalgamated Society of Tailors shows an increase of wages amounting to £40,000 per annum, while the sum spent in strikes and lockouts amounted to only £549 12s. 9d. A great deal of the increase is directly traceable to strikes or threats of strikes; though, of course, part may be due to the general prosperity of the country. Still, it is very doubtful whether the men would have shared in that prosperity had it not been for the existence of the union.

Sir Thomas Brassey's book on *Work and Wages* contains several tables, all showing that wages have increased during past years; and although the fact may not be disputed, it will be well to notice at what rates the increase has been. A few instances from Sir Thomas Brassey's book are therefore given :—

CANADA WORKS, BIRKENHEAD.

Year.			Fitters.			Bricklayers.			Boilermakers	
			s.	d.		s.	d.		s.	d.
1854	...	...	29	0	...	34	0	...	31	6
1856	...	...	29	0	...	34	0	...	30	0
1858	...	...	28	10	...	34	0	...	29	0
1860	...	...	27	6	...	34	0	...	31	0
1862	...	...	27	10	...	34	0	...	31	0
1864	...	...	28	0	...	34	0	...	31	3
1866	...	...	31	0	...	34	0	...	34	2
1868	...	...	31	0	...	34	0	...	32	0
1869	...	...	30	0	...	34	0	...	32	0

IN WALES.

Year.			Miners.	Colliers.	Labourers.
1842	...	...	10s. to 16s.	14s. to 16s.	10s. 6d.
1851	...	...	11s. to 16s.	15s. to 18s.	10s. 6d.
1869	...	...	12s. to 18s.	16s. to 20s.	11s. 6d. to 12s. 6d.

RAILWAYS.

Year.	Masons.		Bricklayers.		Carpenters.		Navvies.	
	s.	d.	s.	d.	s.	d.	s.	d.
1843 ...	21	0 ...	21	0 ...	21	0 ...	16	6
1846 ...	33	0 ...	30	0 ...	30	0 ...	24	0
1851 ...	21	0 ...	21	0 ...	21	0 ...	15	0
1855 ...	25	6 ...	25	6 ...	24	0 ...	19	0
1857 ...	24	0 ...	22	6 ...	22	6 ...	18	0
1863 ...	24	0 ...	24	0 ...	24	0 ...	29	0
1866 ...	27	0 ...	27	0 ...	25	6 ...	20	0
1869 ...	27	0 ...	25	6 ...	24	0 ...	18	0

A more recent table compiled by Mr. Robert Giffen, a most expert statistician, also shows how wages have risen. The table is reproduced here:

Comparison of Wages Fifty Years ago and at Present Time.

Occupation.	Place.	Wages Fifty Years ago, per Week.		Wages Present Time, per Week.		Increase or Decrease, Amount per Cent.		
		s.	d.	s.	d.	s.	d.	
Carpenters	Manchester	24	0	34	0	10	0	(+) 42
,, ...	Glasgow ...	14	0	26	0	12	0	(+) 85
Bricklayers	Manchester*	24	0	36	0	12	0	(+) 50
,, ...	Glasgow ...	15	0	27	0	12	0	(+) 80
Masons	Manchester*	24	0	29	10	5	10	(+) 24
,, ...	Glasgow ...	14	0	23	8	9	8	(+) 69
Miners	Staffordshire	2	8†	4	0†	1	4	(+) 50
Pattern weavers	Huddersfield	16	0	25	0	9	0	(+) 55
Wool scourers ...	,,	17	0	22	0	5	0	(+) 30
Mule spinners ...	,,	25	6	30	0	4	6	(+) 20
Weavers	,,	12	0	26	0	14	0	(+) 115
Warpers and beamers	,,	17	0	27	0	10	0	(+) 58
Winders and reelers	,,	6	0	11	0	5	0	(+) 83
Weavers (men)...	Bradford ...	8	3	20	6	12	3	(+) 150
Reeling and warping...............	,,	7	9	15	6	7	9	(+) 100
Spinning (children)	,,	4	5	11	6	7	1	(+) 160

* 1825.   † Wages per day.

It is worthy of note that the trades selected by Mr. Giffen to establish the fact of an advance of wages are those which have the strongest unions—a circumstance in itself very significant.

It would be easy to prolong the list of these illustrations, were there any need to expatiate on a topic about which there is really no reputable dispute. Hardly a single report is issued by the trade unions that does not call attention to the rise in wages which by combined action has been brought about. Throughout the length and breadth of the land the trade unions have, during the past thirty or forty years, forced wages up, and when wages have fallen, the fall has not been to the low point they were at before the rise began. It would therefore be tedious to fill page after page with a mass of evidence to prove what is universally acknowledged. Wages have risen. That is the great fact. The principal if not the only point upon which discussion arises is as to whether or not the trade unions have assisted to bring about that state of affairs. One thing is certain, the masters are not authorities on the question. They are too crotchety. One of their great arguments against trade unions is that they fail in their object, that they do not succeed in raising wages; while with their next breath they excuse themselves to the public for the high price of coal, by saying " it is the unions raise the price of labour." Perhaps it would be as well if they remembered the experience of the past, when out of eighty strikes for advance of wages forty-three were successful, seven doubtful, and only thirty unsuccessful.

How much of the rise in wages is due to the direct action of trade unions, how much to their indirect action, and how much to general progress and prosperity, are questions that it is difficult, if not impossible to answer. Another table, however, by Mr. Giffen, whom Mr. John Morley describes as "singularly cool and competent," throws a little light upon the subject. It is as follows :—

"Assuming the aggregate income of the people as about 1200 millions now, and that the wages of working men are per head twice what they were, the aggregates in 1843 and at the present time would compare as follows :—

	Income in 1843. Millions.	Income now. Millions.	Increase. Millions.	Increase per cent.
	£	£	£	£
Capitalist classes from capital	190	400	210	110
Working income in Income-tax returns.........	90	180	90	100
Ditto, not in Income-tax returns	235	620	385	160
Total	515	1200	685	130

Thus the increase of what is known as "working-class income" in the aggregate was greater than that of any other class, being 160 per cent., while the return to capital and the return to what are called the "capitalist classes," whether it is from capital proper, or, as Mr. Giffen maintains, a return more in the nature of wages, had only increased about 100 per cent." Can any one for a moment doubt that the "extra" 60 per cent. that fell to the lot of working men is due entirely and solely to the action of trade unions ? Does not all experience show that the capitalist class have ever taken as much as they could ? Had it not been for a resisting influence, and the only resisting influence is the trade union, the figures would have been reversed. The capitalists would have gained an increase of 160 per cent., the operatives of 100. Perhaps the discrepancy would have been much greater. For my own part I believe that trade unions are to be credited with more than 60 per cent. increase, because it would be easy to show that Mr. Giffen has underrated the general increase;* and, as I have already argued, but for the action of the unions there would have been very little advance of wages indeed, nearly all of the increase falling to the capitalist. At any rate 60 per cent. of the 160 per cent. increase must be attributed, and attributed as a minimum, to the direct action of the trade unions.

Although the question, " To what extent is a rise in wages due to the action of a trade union ? " may be difficult to answer, there can be little doubt that some portion of any particular advance is often due to that influence. Where are the masters who ever came forward and advanced wages unasked ? † They are few and far between, and what chance of improving his condition would any labourer have who struck singly ? Very little chance indeed. Now labour, unlike a commodity, will not keep. Once gone, it is gone for ever. A day idly spent is a day lost; and as the capitalist can wait

* " If we had commenced about twenty to twenty-five years ago, we should have been able to show a very great improvement since that time; while at that date also, as compared with an earlier period, a greater improvement would have been apparent." —Mr. Giffen, in the pamphlet already quoted.

† In the Newcastle engineering strike the masters admitted that the condition of trade from the beginning permitted an advance of wages; yet no advance was proposed, till the pressure of the trade unions was brought to bear.

for labour longer than the labourer can wait for wages, there is a natural tendency to depress wages. Then why do they not fall? Is it not because of the counter-acting power of the union? When bricklayers from Liverpool went to work on the new Town Hall at St. Helen's they found men in the same trade as themselves getting higher wages than they were. They instantly demanded to be placed on the same footing as their more fortunate brethren. The masters refused to accede to the request for reasons best known to themselves. A strike ensued, and after a short delay the men accomplished their object. Now, is there one sane man within the four seas of Great Britain who will deny that in this case the Liverpool bricklayers obtained their advance by united action?

This instance shows something more. It shows how, with a widely spread union, the rates of wages in various towns may be known—as in large unions they are—and the highest rate demanded. Had the St. Helen's bricklayers belonged to the same union as those from Liverpool, the difference in the rate of wages in two towns so near each other would have been known and equalized, or, in other words, the lower rate would have been raised. But how can men all over the country ascertain what their labour is worth in various parts of the country unless they act upon the principle of association, and agree upon an organization that encourages an interchange of information between different parts of the country? When, too, the highest rate of wages is discovered, what would be the good of the discovery unless there was a union strong enough to enforce the demands it is desired to make? If not the only way, at any rate the easiest method of ascertaining the "real value "of labour is by putting pressure on the capitalist. Nearly all the present wages rates are based on no real principle of value. Any of the rates are very much below the real value of the work done,* and represent the amount which the workman has been able to squeeze out of his employer, not the full amount to which he is entitled, such amount being all above interest on capital, a charge for deterioration of plant, cost of supervision and cost of conduct of business. In bringing pressure to bear upon the capitalist the union is only doing what merchants and manufacturers do to find out the price of the commodities in which they deal. For two years the attention of the colliery proprietors was chiefly engrossed with "putting on the screw" in greater or less twists at a time, until they found a limit to the disgorging powers of the consumer, and that limit was far beyond the wildest demands ever made by any class of men who have ever struck for an advance of wages. †

But, say those opposed to trade unions, wages would ultimately rise when profits rose, without any combination on the part of the workmen. With a desire to concede as much as possible to our opponents, let us grant this by no means self-evident proposition. There is still the fact that the influence of the union obtains the advance sooner than would otherwise be the case, and that is a gain to the men, and another proof that the societies are able to bring about the results which it

* The wages of the agricultural labourer is an example of this.

† In Manchester the carpenters are paid a halfpenny per hour more than in Liverpool. The reason is stated to be that " in Manchester both employers and employed are thoroughly organized, and an amicable relationship exists between them ; in Liverpool they are comparatively disorganized."

is their object to effect. If there were no combination
amongst the men, and if profits were rising, the masters
would pocket the enhanced profits, until an imperious
necessity obliged them to yield some portion to the starving dependents upon their generosity and benevolence.

Not only, then, is a union able to bring about a rise
in wages sooner than would otherwise be the case, but
it is also able to wrest from the masters a larger share
of the profits than they would concede to a request un-
supported by the power to enforce it. This phase of the
question will be more properly discussed in the next
chapter, and is only mentioned here because some persons imagine all unionists to be " villains of the deepest
dye," and the masters " white-robed innocence from
heaven descended." Such men, amongst a vast amount
of prattle about the identity of the interests of the
employers and employed, are continually suggesting
rose-water remedies as a settlement of a great and
serious question. Their chief advice to the masters is,
" Be kind to your men ; " and to the men, " Trust to
the generosity of your employers." The men, unfortunately, have had a bitter experience of the generosity
from which they are told to expect such great blessings.
They have not yet forgotten the truck system (which
in spite of recent legislation is not yet extinct*), and it
is not so long ago that, to save threepence a day,

* "Truck" shopping is illegal, but it is still practised by
"middle persons," who of course may be summoned before the
magistrates. This, however, is a costly and risky process. The
Leicester Stitchers' and Seamers' Society—a women's union—
recently succeeded in closing nearly all the truck shops by
positively refusing to deal with them. It has cost the little
union a considerable sum of money, which, however, all will
admit was well spent.

masters gave women three shillings a week to stack
large bars of iron, and were only prevented continuing
that policy by the outcry of the public. It is indeed
foolish to maintain that masters would give the full
wages to which men are entitled unless they were forced
to do so. As a matter of fact they have never done so.
On the one hand, in prosperous times they frequently
forget the love professed by them for arbitration when
trade is bad. On the other hand, as Mr. J. D. Prior
pointed out in his presidential address to the Trade
Unions Congress of 1879, the men have on occasions
" taken no advantage of busy years to seek any advance
of wages." The employers, however, will not hesitate
to destroy the reputation of a trade—or for that matter,
as has been well said, of a nation—for the sake of rapid
and increased profits. They are doing so at this moment
at Sunderland, where they show signs that they are
dissatisfied with the non-unionists whom they have
induced to supplant their former workmen. Nearly
every shop is getting work done out of the town which
formerly was done at their own establishments, and
there are other indications that the new class of labour
introduced into the district is such as will very mate-
rially depress the quality of the machines now being
constructed. Masters, as a rule, act in the spirit of
an employer who once said to the author, " That fellow
is worth a pound a week to me, so I give him eighteen
shillings." " Still more," says Mr. J. S. Mill, " might
poor labourers who have to do with rich employers
remain long without the amount of wages which the
demand for their labour would justify, unless, in ver-
nacular phase, they stood out of it ; and how can they
stand out for terms without organized concert ? What

chance would any labourer have who struck singly for an advance of wages? How could he ever know whether the state of the market admitted of a rise, except by consultation with his fellows naturally leading to concerted action?" The only instance that has come under the notice of the author of employers being eager to aid a trade union was recently, when, for their own advantage, they wished to see the resuscitation of the Macclesfield silk weavers' union, as a protection to themselves from each other by equalizing wages, and it is to be hoped the weavers will not allow such an opportunity to pass.

Even if a strike fail, it not only shows that the men have capacity, willingness, and power to combine in such a way that masters will often hesitate ere they resume the encounter; but, paradoxical as it may appear, an unsuccessful strike often succeeds. Suppose there has been a long and terrible dispute, like the one in the agricultural districts, and that those engaged in it have been obliged to return to work without the advance which was at first sought. Can it be doubted that in the case referred to, the praiseworthy pertinacity of the agricultural labourers created such an impression that the farmers will think twice before locking them out when next an advance is asked, especially as all right-feeling and right-thinking men acknowledge that the circumstances of the world are inconsistent with the maintenance of the English agricultural labourer in the condition which has hitherto been his? Or take the case of the London builders, when 10,000 of them gave up £325,000 without at first getting anything for their money, but after they had returned to work "had their wages raised by successive steps from an average

of 25s. to one of 30s., and that without being obliged
to resort to a general strike, or to any strike on a large
scale." All their recent strikes have been what are
termed sectional, and in many instances they have not
had to strike, but have got what they wanted by simply
making it clear that they were prepared to strike unless
they got it. Chiefly by this means it is that they have
succeeded in getting 5s. a week, or 20 per cent., added
to their wages, Now, 5s. a week is £13 a year, which,
multiplied by 10,000, comes to £130,000, or 40 per
cent. on the original outlay, which now yielding such
interest, must be admitted to have been really, in spite
of first appearances, a very tolerable investment.

Indeed, almost the whole of the great failures on the
part of the men, when looked at in the same way, show
that all was not lost—nor, indeed, so much as was supposed. "The same dismal uniformity, the same miserable monotony of defeat," as an ironmaster once called
a long series of strikes, would indeed be gloomy if it
could not be shown that, as in the great Montrose's
campaign, Argyll often gained the victory but failed to
reap its fruits. The great strike of the Manchester
spinners in 1829, when £250,000 of wages were forfeited
apparently to no purpose ; a similar loss when in the
following year 30,000 spinners at Ashton and Staley-
bridge struck work ; the dispute on the Tyne and the
Wear in 1832, when thousands of pitmen held out with
heroic endurance ; the strike of the Manchester builders
in 1833, when £70,000 of wages were sacrificed ; the
Preston strikes in 1836 and 1854, in the former of which
thirteen weeks' idleness cost the men £57,200—and in
the latter there was the terrible suffering of seventeen
thousand persons foregoing £420,000 of wages for

thirty-six weeks; the engineers' strike in 1853, which
lasted fifteen weeks, and in which £43,000 of wages
were lost; the strike in the London building trade in
1860; that of the ironworkers in Staffordshire, and
that in the North in 1865; that of the London tailors
in 1867; and that of the South Wales miners in 1873,
who sacrificed £750,000; to say nothing of the disputes
in the eastern counties, and the numerous disputes and
lock-outs which have recently dotted the island : here
surely (and these are but samples) is a list of failures
sufficient to stamp out the life of unionism, because in
the cases mentioned the men had to give in and return
to work on terms sometimes the same, often worse, and
seldom better, than those against which they struck.
Strikes, however, are sometimes of that nature of which
it can be said, "It is the battle only, and not the victory,
that can be dwelt upon with advantage." The men
often appear to have failed disastrously. But the fact
is, they were not failures entirely. They were defeats in
which the victors got all the glory, the defeated all the
profit. The masters rush to the fight with the dash of
cavalry, and force the men to capitulate; but between
their victories they are constantly giving way to the
men. The workmen seem fully concious of this; and
in a printers' dispute in Liverpool, a few years ago, men
turned out with their fellows when the result of the
former's doing so was to strike for lower wages. Such
was their faith in the ultimate advantages of unionism,
and events showed that they had not miscalculated.
As Mr. Thornton puts it, "During nearly half a century all signal triumphs have been on one side, all
substantial success on the other."

It is not, therefore, just to say that a strike having

cost £700,000 or £800,000, and having failed to obtain that for which it strove, is necessarily a failure. The advance may come later on. Nor can it be said that a strike that has cost £20,000, and raised wages say only £2000, has failed. The strike will certainly have been local; the rise is almost certain to be general. A strike, too, in one portion of the country often enables men to obtain an advance of wages in another portion without recourse to the final appeal. The funds of the union are thus saved, and often a large advance is obtained at a very small cost, as in the case of the tailors in 1873, who, as already mentioned, obtained an advance amounting to £40,000 per annum at a cost of only £594 12s. 9d. A great deal of jubilation was indulged in by the farmers at what they are pleased to call the "failure of the agri-cultural strike." There was, however, little to be proud of in the victory obtained, if a temporary cessation of hostilities could be called a victory. It would be well to remember that the dispute was not a strike at all, but a "lock-out." The farmers of Exning and other places, believing that unionism was a blight and a curse, united themselves, thus showing an inconsist-ency only to be accounted for on the supposition of the Bishop of Manchester that they were going mad. The demand of the men for an advance from thirteen shillings a week to fourteen shillings a week was not thought unreasonable by the masters : it was only the union of the men to which the union of the masters objected. It is well known how master after master at Chevely, Knitling, Stetchworth, Dullingham, Bottis-ham, Alderton, and a score of other parishes, locked out their men—who were not complaining—simply because farmers in other districts locked out theirs.

G

The one condition of working was that the men should leave the union. Every effort was made to induce the masters to deal as honourable and just men should deal. They were asked to surrender nothing but angry feeling. They were called upon to make no sacrifice but that of sentiment. All, however, was in vain ; and a remnant of men were obliged to return to work on the old terms. Can this, however, be called a victory ? Hardly so. Have the farmers stamped out unionism ? Let the National Union, with its 33 districts, 1000 branches, and 20,000 members, answer the question ; and let the Federal Union endorse the answer. Have the farmers succeeded in preventing a rise of wages ? The *Times* says that the wages of agricultural labourers have risen since the unions were formed, but it will not acknowledge that the unions have helped to bring about that advance. On the other hand, the unions have something to show as the result of their efforts. Of the thousands of men locked out, above one-sixth emigrated, and a similar number migrated to where higher wages were to be obtained ; about one-third returned to work without giving up their union tickets ; and the residuum of a few hundreds left the union and returned to work, which is all the "grand result" the masters claim.*

---

* Mr. Wm. Saunders, writing in 1877, said :—"During the last seven years wages have been raised in Wilts and Dorset from 9s. to 12s. per week ; in Norfolk, from 10s. to 13s. ; in Warwickshire, from 9s. to 12s. ; in Lincolnshire, from 12s. to 17s. This increase has been the direct result of trade unionism. It has added one million annually to the wages of the poorest class of our population, and, in doing this, pauperism has been reduced, trade has been improved, the starving poor have been supplied with food, and one of the greatest scandals of our age has been partially removed."

The victory, then, was not much of a thing after all ; and had it been more decisive than it was, would not have been so unsatisfactory. The dispute in the agricultural districts had one feature peculiar to itself. It was not merely a dispute about wages and unionism. The lamentations of the agricultural labourers were a protest against an unjust, a wicked, and a selfish system of land tenure. The fight was against an institution which has long been oppressive, and the farmers of England have done more to bring about a radical reform in the Land Laws of England than the most radical reformers could have accomplished by years of agitation.

"Here's fine revolution, an' we had the trick to see it."

They have done more than this. They have caused colonies of hard-working agricultural labourers to be established in New Zealand, in Australia, and especially in Canada. These men's hearts must naturally be filled with the bitterest feelings. They will educate their children in the belief that their native country "starved them out," and the children of those men who left the Mersey during the agricultural dispute will likely enough be the very men to send a terrible reply to those statesmen who prate about the "integrity of the empire." In 1862 Mr. John Bright saw in his mind's eye that which he expressed in an eloquence and with a boldness peculiarly his own, as " one vast confederation from the frozen north in unbroken line to the glowing south, and from the wild billows of the Atlantic westward to the calmer waters of the Pacific main ; and I see one people, and one language, and one law, and one faith ; and over all that wide continent, the home of freedom, and a refuge for the oppressed of every race and of every clime." Whether that dream will be realized, or whether it should be realized, it would be out of place to mention here. That the question will be discussed is certain, and the farmers of England may take the unction to their souls, that they have greatly helped to bring about that "confederation," by causing to be taken from their native shores those who had suffered so much and endured so long.

What, then, sometimes appears an ineffectual strike often proves to be one of great effect. It must be remembered, too, that non-unionists often reap to some extent the advantages of the unionists. Indeed, in most instances they enjoy all the benefits of an advance brought about by the action of the union, and it is for them to settle with their own consciences the honesty of reaping advantages, to obtain which they have contributed nothing. When they do not obtain the whole of the advantages of a rise, they are pretty sure to obtain some advance, as when the "standard" of wages has been raised it drags after it a general increase all round. It appears from this that union workmen are perfectly justified in refusing to work with non-union men, though the practice of doing so is far from general. The latter have done nothing to raise or sustain wages, and ought not to expect to enjoy the results of the sacrifices, the moral courage, and the contributions of the unionists. Whenever union workmen do work with non-union men it shows that unselfishness and generosity—that sinking of self for others—which are characteristic of almost all unions. It is worth mentioning, too, that other trades besides the one "on strike" are often benefited by an advance in the wages of those "on strike." Thus, if the "puddlers" receive an advance of wages, the hammermen, the rollers, and the labourers are pretty certain to be similarly treated. It is thus seen that the material advantages of a strike cannot be reckoned by taking the cost of the strike and the gain in wages, and subtracting one from the other.

It may be said—and very justly—that, if the general tendency of trade unionism be to raise wages, then, where there are no unions, wages should be lower than ordinary. This is exactly the case. Unfortunately, the non-unionists keep no statistics, and it is impossible to ascertain the exact wages they are paid. It is, however, generally known that the worst paid trades in the kingdom are those which have no unions. The evidence of the men themselves is valuable on this point, because, unless they felt they received an advantage, they would leave the union. What the men want is high wages for little work, as much wages as they can get for as little work as they can do, and if their unions could not give those benefits to them they would cease to support them. "I have been a worker," says one operative, "something like forty-four years. For twenty years of that period I have been employed in erecting machinery in different parts of the country, and I have no hesitation in saying, wherever we find union principles ignored a low rate of wages prevails, and the reverse where organization is perfect. The most approved remedy for low wages is combination." The Aldershot shoemaking trade was some time ago " scratched " when the masters were instantly enabled to reduce the wages of their men one shilling per pair.

An advance of wages, however, is not the only object of a trade union, nor the sole purpose of a strike. Sometimes the men demand shorter hours. To work a

less number of hours for the same amount of wages is
naturally attractive to the workman. He not only sees
that such an arrangement gives him more time for
recreation and for the enjoyment of home comforts—for
billiards, books, or beer—without calling on his wife to
"pinch, cut, and contrive," but that the reduction of
hours causes more of his fellow-workmen to be employed.
The demand for a commodity being the same, and the
number of working hours diminished, more men must
be employed to produce the same amount of work in
less time. Men who were forced to be idle are thus
provided with employment. These additional workmen
become spenders as well as producers, and the advantages
of that he knows to consist in a general improvement
all round. In thus benefiting himself, therefore, he is
benefiting his class. Of course, it may be argued that
this reasoning might be applied to a reduction of hours
ad finitum, until the differential calculus were required
to ascertain the moments men should work. It may be
said that the reasons recently urged for and against the
Nine Hours Bill were simply repetitions of those urged
in 1846 on either side when the Ten Hours Bill was
before the country; and that, for anything now known,
may be again set forth in favour of an Eight Hours
Bill in 1886, and a Seven Hours Bill in 1900. About five
times in a century, masters imagine, an hour a day may
be lopped off, until men will work only one hour *per diem*,
at full weekly wages, and then "What will become of the
country?" This is, of course, the tendency, and would
indeed be the result, if matured and competent artisans
were rained down from heaven in myriads, instead of
being born individually in a state of puny infancy, unfit
for anything but to be "fretted with sallies of their

mothers' kisses." Under the existing state of affairs
there is no cause for alarm in this respect any more
than there is for the fear felt by the late Mr. Dennys,
author of "Alpha," who argued that trade unions
"could gain nothing by their crusade against low wages
if every workman were a unionist, for the result would
be high wages triumphant, but no one to pay them—a
successful organization of the workmen, but no work."
There is an obvious fallacy in the argument. A strong
trade union is powerful, but it is not omnipotent. No
union could force wages up to such a pitch that employers would receive no profit on their capital expenditure. The greatest unanimity among workmen could
only obtain such wages as the capitalist could afford to
pay. The present grievance is that this high point has
never yet been reached, and employers, therefore, appropriate not only interest on their capital, but a portion
of the operatives' wages as well. There is an opposing
tendency to this continual reduction of hours and
advancement of wages. The amount of commodity
that shall be produced does not depend upon the will
either of the capitalist or the labourer. Come what
will, men will be fed and clothed by hook or by crook,
and the more wages they have the better, and the more
abundant will their food and clothing be. Some men,
therefore, *must* produce. An imperious necessity demands it. The tendency of a Factory Act, or rather of
the reduction in the number of working hours, is to
force a greater number of men into the producing class.
As the demands of the world increase, this tendency
becomes stronger. The number of producers, however,
is after all limited, and there is therefore a point beyond
which neither a trade union nor the Legislature could

be successful in attempting to reduce the number of
hours.   This point is determined by the amount to be
produced and the number of producers.   Hitherto the
masters have made a profit by keeping the men from
this point.   For some time the men have struggled to
reach it, and although they may not yet have done so,
yet the Legislature has stepped in, and given such an
instalment that as soon as the present block to parliamentary business is removed, there is every reason to
believe that the demands of the Trade Union Congress
for an Eight Hours Bill will be readily granted.   For
the victory of the past great credit is due to Mr. Mundella, who, although an employer, is yet able to see that
in benefiting the labouring class he is not injuring his
own.   "It is best," said he, "to concentrate labour into
as few hours as possible."   Mr. Hugh Mason and other
employers, especially in the cotton districts, take a
similar view of the question, and maintain that shorter
hours by no means signify less production; and facts
have been quoted by them which strengthen an argument which will be used further on in these pages.

The above proposition, stated in general terms, is of
course true in particular instances.   It would, however,
be an insult to the intelligence of the reader if special
applications were made to particular trades.   It is quite
evident that if all the weavers of a certain material be
employed full time at full wages, and that the consumption of the commodity is proceeding as rapidly as its
production, there can be no reduction of hours without
injury to the community at large.

No action of the trade unionists has been crowned
with such signal success as that taken to bring about
the reduction of hours.   The State itself watched the

straining efforts that were being made, both recently
and in years gone by; and when there was a sign
of tottering or failure, came to its assistance. "The
demand is against the laws of political economy," cry
the masters. "We ask a blessing," reply the men,
"but are not strong enough to force it." So Parliament steps in and gives a Factory Act; just as when the
men (not the masters) complained that their union was
not strong enough to better the condition of miners
when underground, the House of Commons passed a
"Mines Regulation Act." The support which the demands of the unions are receiving from Parliament is a
very significant phenomenon in the history of England.

What is very surprising is that the masters believe
that they can get more work out of a man when they
work him to death. They forget that it is not the
miles one travels, but the pace that kills. They ignore
the doctrine of Adam Smith, that "the man who works
so moderately as to be able to work constantly, not
only preserves his health the longest, but in the course
of the year executes the greatest quantity of work."
Capitalists do not pursue such a policy in regard to
their horses. The fact is, they are not thinking of
their men. They are brooding over their valuable
machinery standing idle, and calculating what it would
bring them if it went on working a few hours longer.
The manufacturer sitting in his counting-house, within
sound of the murmur of his machinery and the chink-
ing of his engine, hums to himself at each clack of the
fly-wheel, "So much for me, so much for me." And
when he beholds his "hands" leaving for home on a
summer evening while it is yet light, and no longer hears
the heavy beat of the beam or the rattle of the shuttle,

he looks upon the stillness as the symbol of his loss. Such men must be very miserable on Sundays.

It is now, however, a well ascertained fact that, within certain limits, more work is done as a rule where there is a prospect of an early cessation from work than when men know that they are doomed to several hours of continuous employment. A few years ago the average day's work in England was ten hours. On the Continent it was twelve, in Russia sixteen or seventeen; and yet it is calculated that two English mowers would do in a day the work of six Russian ones. Russian factory operatives worked seventy-five hours in the week, when those in England worked only sixty, yet the work of the former was only one-fifth of that of the latter. When the average working time of a miner in South Wales was twelve hours a day those in the North of England worked only seven, yet the cost of getting coals in Aberdare was 25 per cent. more than in Northumberland. As has been well said, "The workman who cannot tire himself in eight hours is not worth his salt."

There are several other objects for which men strike or are locked out. The nature of this treatise, however, is too general to admit of their peculiarities being inquired into or their merits discussed. It is sufficient to say that when men strike it is "to better their condition," or to demand something which they think will have that result. Some persons object on principle to "piece-work." A little consideration, however, shows that such a system may be right— nay, must be right—in some trades, while payment by the hour may be equally just in others. Surely the task of watching machines, the production of which never varies, can be paid for by the day, but occupations upon which the amount produced depends upon the industry of the operative ought certainly to be paid by the piece. The justice of this is so patent that it would be a sign of obtuseness on the part of the men if they could not show that piece-work is the general rule in almost every trade with the exception of the building and engineering, and it must be mentioned that in the former the masters are agreed with the men on the point.

In showing the efficacy of trade unions, and in maintaining the justice of their demands, it must not be thought that the author imagines they never err. No one will pretend to deny that the unions have done what many people do not approve, and which they themselves, on calmer reflection, do not approve. But this, as Mr. Bright says, only shows they are not immaculate, and that their wisdom, like that of other classes, is not perfect. One is tired of hearing that the result of trade unions was Broadhead, Crookes, and Hallam; that its means were ruffianism and murder; its ends never inquired into. These men were not the result of unionism, but of the attempt to crush unionism.* The laws of the country made all unionists conspirators. Even the simplest actions, which are now allowable, were illegal, and when what is morally right is decided by tribunals to be legally wrong, the culprit has more respect for himself than he has for the law. Unionism, however, needs no defence here

---

* Broadhead himself said to the Royal Commissioners: "If the law would only give the unions some power to recover contributions, without having recourse to such measures, there would be no more heard of them."

on this head. The press may croak about the three
miscreants above named until it is hoarse; it can have
little effect upon an institution which has produced
such men as Thomas Burt, Henry Broadhurst, William
Allan, John Burnett, Joseph Arch, and John Kane.

At the same time the unions, and especially the
union secretaries, have a very difficult task to perform.
The average British workman · is not yet sufficiently
advanced in intelligence to apprehend that wages may
vary in two ways. His union, it is imagined, has
power to force wages up; he is loth to admit that it
cannot sometimes resist their falling. The author
once saw an ironworker who had been dismissed from
his work because he had been drinking for three days;
and the stupid fellow was very wroth indeed because
the union secretary would not order a strike on account
of the man's dismissal. "I pay my money to t'
union," said he, "for protection, and this is how you
serve me." The executive of a union, then, has to be
careful, not only that it does not strike unless it has
right on its side, but it has to educate the men to
the same opinion. The workmen have to be taught
that they must not attempt to obtain from capital
impossible concessions. They must only strike when
cessation of production means loss of profit to the
masters. For instance, it would not only be mani-
festly unjust but absurd to strike for higher wages
in the face of a falling market. How difficult it is
to impress this upon the men the union secretary knows
full well. Sometimes the men cannot see the force
of the forbearance which is urged upon them, and in
their ignorance are very self-willed. It cannot be forgotten how Mr. Pickard and other leaders recommended

the men of St. Helen's and Wigan in 1862 to accept
an inevitable reduction of 15 per cent., how that advice
was spurned by men who, in their fury, actually seized
the Wigan Iron and Coal Company's works, and kept
them several days, until the military were called out.
The Lancashire operatives a few months ago (1883–84)
would have done well to have followed the advice of
their leaders, but excepting that instance and some
other occasions, the men are showing more intelligence
on this point. To a large extent this is due to the
great and deserved influence of Mr. Burt, Mr. Macdonald, Mr. John Kane, Mr. Halliday, Mr. Thomas
Birtwistle, and Mr. John Burnett.

It is gratifying to find that greater care than formerly
is taken to prevent those strikes which, being foolish,
were always disastrous. How easily this may be done
is evident from the practice in some trades of keeping complete registers in which the fluctuations of the
market are indicated, and the union secretaries are
as well acquainted with the price of cotton and iron as
the masters. Even this, however, is not always sufficient, and the masters show, with arguments seemingly
plausible, that their profits are very small. The men,
however, though unable to point out the fallacy in the
reasoning opposed to them, nevertheless are aware of
its existence. "We have been working at a loss for
years," said a large cotton manufacturer to the union
secretary. "Yes," was the shrewd reply, "you have
been losing your little mills and building bigger ones."
The cotton spinners of Bolton, in September, 1874, sent
a similar reply to the notice of a reduction of wages
given by the masters. "The operatives," said the reply,
"cannot judge of trade from your standpoint. They

draw conclusions from circumstantial evidence, and contend that the princely fortunes that seem to be amassed around us cannot have arisen from an unremunerative business; therefore you must pardon them if it be difficult to make them believe that a reduction in wages is called for."

It would, indeed, solve this great question if some infallible authority were appealed to who could decide what was a fair day's wages for a fair day's work, instead of leaving its discovery to the bitter struggle between the undue forcing up of wages on the one hand and the unduly depressing of them on the other. That there is such a "rate of wages" is undoubtedly true, and it was a gross blunder on the part of a writer in the *Beehive*, then the organ of the trade unions, to deny this in some foolish criticisms on a very excellent speech made by Mr. Thomas Burt in Wales, in July, 1874. The honourable member for Morpeth, with a fearless fairness and a force peculiarly his own, denounced the practice of forcing wages higher than their "natural rate," upon which the *Beehive* maintained that the "natural rate" was as much as a man could get. Experience ought to have taught the editor of the *Beehive* that as much as a man can get is often *less* than the "natural rate." The agricultural labourers eleven years ago showed a determination to increase their wages, and they had to return to work very little if at all better in this respect than when the dispute began. No one will have the fortitude to maintain that the agricultural labourers were being paid their natural and proper rate of wages, and yet they were receiving as much as they could get. A fair rate of wages is as much or as little as a man ought to get; and if the writer understood Mr. Burt rightly, that gentleman wished to impress upon his hearers that men could not get more than they were entitled to without keeping a certain number of themselves permanently idle. It is certainly a fair question for discussion whether or not the rate of wages at the present day is as high as it ought to be, even in the best paid trades. Capital is increasing far faster than population. When the latter had doubled itself the former had quadrupled itself. It seems, therefore, merely obedience to a natural law that wages should rise ; and if trade unions have failed in their efforts at all, it is in the fact that while they have raised wages, they have not raised them enough.

There is another consideration under this head. A strike at the wrong time may not only fail in its attempt to raise wages—it may prevent a rise. Happily instances of this are extremely rare, but as Mr. Rupert Kettle has imagined one, it may be useful to give the instance, and in his own words :—" A particular trade may be very active, with an unusual demand for operatives in Surreysex, but in its ordinary state, or perhaps rather flat, in Umbershire. To improve the condition of the men in Umbershire the union orders a rise in wages or a strike there, and trade in that district being in its normal state only, wages cannot he raised, therefore an alternative must be resorted to, and the men moved to Surrreysex. In Surreysex they are offered to the masters to satisfy the extraordinary local demand there, and so wages are prevented from rising in the place to which men are taken. Let us see " (continues Mr. Kettle) " how the market would have righted itself if the union had not interfered. As the masters in Surreysex wanted them, unless men came and offered

to work, they would have had to seek them and to bid
for them. It would then be to the seller and not the
buyer to whom the inducement to deal must be held
out. If the labourers from Umbershire must be brought
by inducement to Surreysex, the masters must bring
them by giving an advanced price. When the Surreysex master offered his advance to the Umbershire men
their home master would be there to bid against him,
and then the Surreysex buyer must make a further
advance. Whatever rise was thus obtained would be
general both in the one locality and the other, so long as
the extra demand lasted. It is thus the union plan of
stopping work in one place, and so throwing labour
upon the market in another, where it is in great demand,
has the effect of checking a rise by forcing men to bid
for the masters instead of waiting quietly—like good
marketers—until the masters bid for the men." Although this is a supposititious case, yet it is somewhat
similar in principle to what has actually taken place in
some disputes between miners and their employers in
the west of England and in the north of Scotland. It
was with a recollection of this that Mr. Macdonald at
Dunfermline counselled the miners to return to work
even at a loss rather than prolong the struggle. "It
would be a thousand times better," said he, "to submit
to a reduction of even 40 per cent., rather than bring
upon themselves the disastrous effects of the strikes in
the north of England and the west of Scotland, which
had ruined the union, and had resulted in the men
now working at even lower wages."

A tribunal to fix or discover a definition of a "fair
day's wages" was hinted at in a preceding paragraph.
The combination of the masters to "meet" the combi-

nations of the men are preparing the way for such a tribunal, though the bitter hostility and the savage feeling which some masters have often displayed oblige us to believe that the day of fair bargaining is not so nigh as is wished. It reflects great credit upon the men that they exhibit a desire to deal fairly with those combinations of masters, which seem to have been formed more for the express purpose of insulting the men and their unions than for any sensible or legitimate object. The men have always approved of unions amongst employers, believing that by such means the labour question stands a better chance of settlement than it ever had before. *Capital and Labour* often blames the men for combining to force wages up, but it has not a word to say against the masters for combining to force wages down. The editor of that paper seldom neglects to inform his readers when a miner makes a book on the Derby, gives £50 for a dog, or mistakes his master for a groom. He is, however, silent on the vices of the capitalist. Masters who, living under the Tudors, copied their despotism, could hardly have demanded more concessions from their men than did the West Suffolk Farmers' Defence Association. They asked that the men should give up their liberty. The "striking" power must be done away with : the union must be "demolished ;" "the voices of Mr. Arch, Mr. Taylor, and Mr. Ball no more heard, and—are we in England ?—the *Union Chronicle* suppressed "—before the high and mighty farmers would, as they boasted, even negotiate, much less yield; while almost all the farmers' unions pledged themselves "never to employ another union man on any consideration." Imagine the men making similar demands ! Suppose Mr. Arch

H

going to the West Suffolk farmers, and saying to them,
" Gentlemen, when you cease to combine and to have
the power of locking-out; when the Marquis of Bristol
and Mr. Hunter Rodwell, Q.C., speak no more; and
when you no longer derive your inspiration from the
leading columns of the *Standard*, but regularly imbibe
the weekly wisdom of the *Labourers' Union Chronicle*—
then, Mr. Farmer, we will negotiate with you, and tell
you what we want, but not till then." Surely common
sense and the true British love of fair play must allow
such demands to proceed from the men as much as from
the masters! Members of the masters' unions have
shown a more inveterate spirit even in their individual
capacity than in their collective character. The conduct of the Halberton farmers towards Canon Girdle-
stone shows that they were equal to Broadhead, Hallam,
and Crooke in everything but pluck. They insulted
their pastor's wife and children when they met them on
the road; they hissed him down when he tried to speak
in the vestry; they swore at him and about him; and
in every way they could think of showed to him and
the world what a set of mean, ruffianly miscreants they
were. It is indeed very questionable whether any
intelligent man in this country could have possibly
imagined that there was so much baseness latent in the
British farmer, until it displayed itself in such vast
proportions during the Eastern counties dispute. The
following is taken from the *Daily News* :—

" Farmer (to one of his labourers, a ' likely ' lad of
seventeen) : ' George, they tell me you are going off to
the north.'

" George : ' Well, zur, you see I be working here for
nine shillings a week, and I am told I could get twelve

shillings or fourteen shillings if I leave feyther and go to farm up in——.'

"Farmer : ' Your father, George, has worked on the farm, man and boy, for forty years, and he has had good wages; and, if he don't get much now, you know that, what with his rheumatiz and his bad foot, he don't do much work; but he lives in one of my cottages, and your mother and all of you—and you know your mother can't do much, and your lame sister is not worth much neither; and I tell you what, George, if you be going, why, God damn my eyes, I speak true, the whole lot of you—father, mother, and brats and all—they shan't stay a day behind you.   There ! ' "

This conversation is said actually to have taken place. The bitterness of spirit which displays itself in the breasts of the masters is not confined to farmers.   It is not so very long ago that an Ayrshire colliery owner not only refused to employ unionists, but forbade his men attending meetings or asking others to do so, under no less a penalty than being summoned for a " breach of agreement according to law," which shows the spirit in which he interpreted the " Criminal Law Amendment Act."   In February, 1874, a man was dismissed in Scotland for collecting subscriptions towards Mr. A. Macdonald's election expenses.   Mr. T. J. Dunning, in his excellent pamphlet, as well as other writers, gives worse instances than the above, and indeed few persons know the insults to which workmen are subjected.

There is, however, a better and more hopeful prospect ahead, because the masters are now recognizing the unions of the men, and are gradually discontinuing the abuse with which hitherto they have been so lavish.   And in sooth it should be so, as the masters'

combinations stigmatizing the men's unions by oppro-
brious epithets is very much like the pan calling the
kettle black. No trade union has ever had such pre-
tentious objects as have the masters' combinations.
The Yorkshire and Derbyshire coal-owners meet, not
only to decide upon the rate of wages they will pay,
but even to dictate the price of coal. In 1864 one
combination of masters assisted men on strike against
another combination of masters. Trade unions, however, have always been true to themselves. They have
never colleagued with masters against their fellow-
workmen. Masters, even knowing and acknowledging
that they were in the wrong, have not hesitated to lock
out their men because some of their own union had
decided to lock out theirs. As an instance, there is the
tailors' strike in 1866. The great point, however, with
which masters' associations have troubled themselves,
and which they will have to face more and more, is the
policy they sometimes pursue of each master not competing with his neighbour for labour, thus raising its
price, but by a strict and rigid combination doing all
they can to force it to the lowest possible point.

War is essentially such an uncongenial state of
affairs that no surprise can be felt that the combinations of masters and of men endeavour to discover
some means of amicably settling disputes. It would
naturally suggest itself to minds on both sides that a
meeting of ambassadors or delegates from the men
should meet similar officers from the masters to talk
over matters. That this should come about was pro-
phesied so long ago as 1846 by Mr. John Bright, who,
in opposing the Factory Bill, said that "the working
classes would every day become more and more power-

ful and intelligent—not by violent combinations or
collisions with their employers, but by a rational union
amongst themselves, by reasoning with their employers,
and by the co-operation of all classes." It is worth
noting that the initiatory step in this direction was
taken by the trade unions. The late general secretary
of the Amalgamated Society of Engineers, over and
over again, during many years, advocated what is
known now as "arbitration," and he was ably backed
in his efforts by Mr. R. Applegarth, late secretary of
the Amalgamated Society of Carpenters, and other
well-known trade unionists. In 1860 a board of arbitration was formed, *at the request of the men*, amongst
the Nottingham lace-workers, and since then the
trades of Staffordshire, Middlesborough, Cleveland,
Bradford, Sheffield, and other places have followed
that example.

It would be out of place here to point out upon what
bases arbitrations should be formed. Mr. Rupert
Kettle, in his pamphlet, has provided us with the
necessary forms of proceeding. It is sufficient to state
that such a mode of settling a dispute ought always to
be encouraged. It is very much cheaper to both sides
than a strike or a lock-out; and it does not leave behind
it that "immortal hate and study of revenge" which
are the result—in the present state of human nature—
of a long and rancorous struggle. The argument that
an arbitration is useless because it is not binding in law
is neither true in fact nor just in reason. The contract
which Mr. Kettle directs to be signed when he acts as
arbitrator is as binding as any other contract, but if it
were not, honour has such force in our public code of
morality that both masters and men would feel bound

to obey a compact solemnly and freely entered into. It is urged by some that arbitrations are unjust in principle because they are founded upon a fallacy, viz. that they can fix the future market price of labour, irrespective of the laws of supply and demand. This, however, is not so. To fix the price of labour for a certain time —for so many weeks, or so many days—in advance is not deciding upon a future price. It is merely selling a larger quantity of labour at to-day's price, or, as Mr. Kettle puts it, of " to-day's labour." It is generally better in all commodities—better for both buyer and seller—to deal wholesale. The masters will buy no more of labour at a higher price than they can help; the men will sell as little at a low price as they possibly can. To say that such a contract as the one here supposed decides the future price of labour is no more true than that a man agreeing to supply another man with apples at twopence a pound for six months is deciding upon a future price for apples. The price is to-day's price, the other article in the agreement relates merely to the times of delivery. Perhaps in arbitrations may be seen what will one day become an impartial tribunal for determining what is a " fair day's wages for a fair day's work," and it is one of the best, as it is one of the most gratifying proofs of the efficacy of trade unions, that they have been so successful in the formation of boards of arbitration, and in teaching their men to submit to the decision of the arbitrators.

In order, however, that trade unions may lay claim to fitness for carrying out their objects, they must show something more than that they are able to conduct a strike to a successful issue, to palliate the evils of an unsuccessful strike, and to succeed in occasionally form-

ing a board of arbitration. They must show that in
their very nature they have the desire and the power to
prevent strikes. It is gratifying to be able to state that
in this respect, also, the trade unions are eminently
successful. Indeed economy, if nothing else, would
dictate such a policy. The executories of trade unions
have been taught by experience that, even when an
object is worth striving for, a strike is often the worst,
and always the most expensive, way of obtaining it.
Strikes, as a rule, are a *dernier ressort*, and are more
frequently discountenanced by the general secretary
than approved of by him. Indeed, it is the boast of
most trade union secretaries that they have prevented
more strikes than they have originated. This is all the
more creditable, because some branch or other is always
urging a strike. " At least twenty times in as many
months," wrote Mr. Allan, " we have recommended that
a strike should not take place." " About one-third,"
answered Mr. Applegarth, when questioned on the subject by the Royal Commissioners, " of the applications
made to us to strike during the last few years have been
refused ; " and Mr. Macdonald, secretary of the House
Painters' Alliance, said—" Our parent society never
originated a strike, but it has stopped many." The
desire of the trade unionists to prevent strikes is also
shown by the following resolution, which was unanimously agreed upon at the Trade Unions' Congress in
1874, viz. :—"That in the opinion of this congress, that
in all trades where disputes occur, and where it is
possible to prevent strikes by starting co-operative
establishments, all trades societies and trades councils
be recommended to render such assistance as lies in
their power, and thus, as far as possible, prevent strikes

and lock-outs in the future." This, at any rate, shows that the unions are as willing to devote their funds to the prevention of strikes as to their origination; and although some of the speakers to that resolution showed a preference for co-operative principles, inconsistent with a thorough belief in those of trade unionism, yet the congress wisely limited its resolution to those circumstances when the co-operative form of trading is certain to prevent a strike, and not to the promulgation of co-operative principles generally.*

The accounts of the various trade unions, also, shows how reluctant the executories are to indulge in the luxury of a strike. This was recently pointed out by Mr. George Howell, in his clever and concise article in the *Contemporary Review* of September, 1883, and by Mr. Frederic Harrison in his address at the Trade Union Congress at Nottingham in the following month, published in the same magazine in November last. Attention has been already called to this subject on pp. 54, *et seq.*, but the passage will bear repetition. " Last year," says Mr. Frederic Harrison, " the Amalgamated Engineers, with an income of £124,000 and a cash balance of £168,000, expended in disputes altogether, including the support they gave to other trades, £895 only. That was far less than one per cent. of the whole of their income. The ironfounders spent, out of an income of £42,000, £214 only; and the Amalgamated Carpenters, who had had a number of disputes and been engaged in strikes, spent £2000 out of £50,000, which was only four per cent. The tailors, with £18,000, spent £565 only; and the stonemasons, with 11,000 members in union, spent nothing in strikes. During six years of

* See pp. 148 *et seq.*

unexampled bad trade, and reduction of wages, and industrial disturbance, there were a great many strikes, and during that period seven great trade societies expended in the settlement of disputes £162,000 only out of a capital of nearly £2,000,000. Last year (1882) these societies, with an aggregate income of £330,000 and a cash balance of £360,000, expended altogether in matters of dispute about £5000, which was not two per cent. on the whole of their income, and not one per cent. on their total available resources for the year." When it is remembered that 99 per cent. of these societies' expenditure were for benevolent and provident purposes and one per cent. only for strikes, it is absurd to say that the chief object of a trade union is to foster trade disputes.

The power on the part of trade unions to prevent strikes increases with the strength of the unions. One of the most pleasing features in unionism is that the most powerful associations show least inclination to strike. Where the power to do evil is greatest, the will to use that power is least. Strength has been accompanied by intelligence and discretion. The Glassmakers' Society is composed of every man in the trade, and has, therefore, so to speak, an entire monopoly; and yet, strange and gratifying to relate, they seldom have any dispute. The masters frequently consult with the representatives of the union, and if the former wish to engage additional hands they communicate with the atter, and men are instantly found. It is to be hoped that the facts to which attention is here directed will be sufficient to remove the hatred to unionism of those who believe that trade unions are the cause of strikes. A union does, indeed, render a strike possible, but it

cannot cause one.   As has been aptly said, to maintain
that unions are the cause of strikes is the same as
saying that gunpowder is the cause of war.   It is,
indeed, the kind of reasoning used by Jedediah Cleish-
botham in introducing Mr. Pattison's MS. to the
public—

> "That without which a thing is not
> Is *causa sine qua non*."

There were strikes before there were trade unions, and
it is a fact worth remembering that the most violent
strikes have been where unions did not exist.

Perhaps, however, the strongest argument in favour
of the efficacy of trade unionism is the rapidity with
which its principles are spreading amongst the working
men.   If unionism did not benefit the working man—
did not, that is, carry out its object—the working man
would leave it ; and were not the advantages he receives
of a very definite and material nature, he would not
submit to the heavy tax upon his wages which his
society demands—a tax considerably more than half
of the amount demanded from him by the Imperial
Exchequer.   The men, however, do not leave the union.
In 1859 it was estimated that the number of members
of trade unions was 600,000; in 1870 it had, it was
calculated, increased to 800,000.   In 1874 I estimated
the number at 1,500,000; and two years later Mr.
George Howell fixed the membership of the different
societies at 1,600,000.   All these figures, however,
were avowedly guesses, and were exaggerations.   The
organization of the Trade Unions' Congress gives us now
a basis on which to make some sort of calculation.   At
the last conference there were 173 delegates, from 135
bodies, representing 561,091 persons.   I estimate that

the number of trade unionists at the present time does not exceed 800,000. It is, however, rapidly increasing. In 1870 Mr. Thornton estimated that only about 10 per cent. of the workmen were members of unions, but he added that "at the present rate of proselytism it will take but few years more for all eligible workmen in this country to become converts to unionism, and enrolled members of trade societies." Since Mr. Thornton wrote the "rate of proselytism" has wonderfully increased. The Agricultural Labourers' Unions have both sprung into existence since 1870, while the larger unions have considerably increased in number of members. The Amalgamated Society of Engineers increased in 1883 alone by 2030 members, the Amalgamated Carpenters by 2274 in the last four years, the United Society of Boilermakers and Iron Shipbuilders by 12,558 in the last four years. Last year the Amalgamated Society of Railway Servants added no less than 1756 names to its list of members, and other associations have increased in like proportion. The five largest societies have doubled the number of their members in sixteen years. There are, however, upwards of six millions of working men in the United Kingdom. Rapid as has been the progress of trade unionism, there is, therefore, ample room for further development. Indeed, trade unions are as yet in their infancy. They recognize this, and many of them are exercising themselves to bring non-unionists to see the wisdom of entering their portals. It is to be hoped their efforts will be crowned with success, and that in a very few years every working man will belong to the union of his trade.

Years ago trade unions were considered too insig-

nificant for notice. The Press entirely ignored them,
and publishers refused to print literature concerning
them. When their existence was at last recognized,
they were treated with an uncompromising hostility
—they were regarded as enemies to social order and
progress. To be a trade unionist was to be a "dangerous character," and that trade unions ought to be
suppressed was the general opinion of what is called
the respectable portion of the community. All this is
now changed ; trade unions are not only acknowledged
to be justifiable, but necessary. Magazine editors throw
open their pages to the unions' champions, and even
the trade union secretaries themselves contribute articles
to the leading publications of the day. The representatives of unions hold converse with Cabinet ministers,
and the assistance of the societies is eagerly sought by
candidates for parliamentary honours. The proceedings
of the congresses are telegraphed from one end of the
kingdom to the other. Unions are now acknowledged
as a power for "good," and, to crown all, they have
succeeded in placing three of their secretaries in the
House of Commons itself, and there is every likelihood,
ere long, of many more being returned as members of
that assembly.

It was discovered that what unionists wanted was
not to rob capital, but obtain for labour its rights. It
was hoped that the employers would see the question
in this light ; and one of the most distressing features
in the discussion of this question is the violent hostility,
the determination to fight, the desire for war, displayed
in the programme of "The National Federation of
Associated Employers of Labour." That document,
however, testifies to the power and efficacy of trade

unions, which is the point at present under consideration. Amidst a good deal of misrepresentation the
employers acknowledge that the unionists have an
"elaborate organization." "Few are aware," they
say, "of the extent, compactness of organization, large
resources, and great influence of trade unions. They
have an annual congress at which an increasing number
of unions are represented each year." "They have the
control of enormous funds, which they expend freely
in furtherance of their objects, and the proportion of
their earnings which the operatives devote to the service
of their leaders is startling." We should think so, to
the mind of a selfish master. The associations "are
federated together, acting in common accord under able
leaders." "They have a well-paid and ample staff of
leaders, most of them experienced in the conduct of
strikes, many of them skilful as organizers, all forming
a class apart, a profession, with interests distinct from,
though not necessarily antagonistic to, those of the
workpeople they lead." "They have, through their command of money, the imposing aspect of their organization, and partly, also, from the mistaken humani-
tarian aspirations of a certain number of literary men
of good standing [sic 'mistaken' men, i.e. such as the
late J. S. Mill, Prof. Beesley, Frederic Harrison, Henry
Crompton, W. T. Thornton, and others], a large array
of literary talent, which is prompt in their service on
all occasions of controversy. They have their own
Press as a field for those exertions. Their writers have
free access to some of the leading London journals.
They organize frequent meetings at which paid speakers
inoculate the working classes with their ideas, and urge
them to dictate terms to candidates for Parliament. . . .

They have a standing Parliamentary Committee, and a programme, and active members of Parliament are energetic in their service. They have the attentive ear of the minister of the day, and their communications are received with instant and respectful attention. [The masters are galled.] They have a large representation of their own body in London whenever Parliament is likely to be engaged in the discussion of the proposals they have caused to be brought before it. Thus, untrammelled by pecuniary considerations, and specially set apart for this peculiar work, without other clashing occupations, they resemble the staff of a well-organized, well-provisioned army, for which everything that foresight and preoccupation in a given purpose could provide is at command. . . . These results are the deserved reward of the superiority of the trade unionists over the employers in those high qualities of foresight, generalship, and present self-sacrifice, for the sake of future advantage [what an admission!], which form necessary elements in the success of every organized society." Truly, if there were any doubts as to the fitness of trade unions to attain their objects, the National Federation of Associated Employers of Labour has removed that doubt. Have the trade unions succeeded? Ask the federated employers. There can be no better proof, not only of the power, but of the justice of trade unionism, than the document from which the above quotations are taken.

Although, then, trade unions have proved themselves thoroughly fit and able to carry out the main objects for which they were formed, yet it cannot be denied that, in regard to one portion of their programme, they have not shown the same tact and ability. There is the authority of the chief actuaries in the country for saying that the insurance funds—as they may be called —of some of the trade unions are based upon false data. The amounts expended under this head are for sickness, superannuation, accidents, funerals, etc., and the sum total thus expended is very large, in some instances much greater than is spent in conducting a strike or opposing a lock-out.* As has been already pointed out, such benevolent notions had very little to do with the formation of a union. They were mere subterfuges tacked to the charter of a union because it was illegal for them to exist without them. When they were "registered," however, they had a sort of quasi-legal existence, and could, at any rate, meet legally. It is probable that the care and attention of the original members would be devoted more to the immediate advantage of increased wages than in calculating premiums for a sick and burial fund. Probably, also, the actuarial abilities of the first promoters of unions were not very great. At any rate, there is the fact that in respect to that portion of a union which resembles a "friendly society," there is, as a rule, a great degree of unsoundness. The sooner this is altered the better;† and perhaps it would not be amiss if steps

* The seven largest unions spent £220,095 in 1881 in the above-named benefits.

† In 1869 the Trade Union Commissioners recommended an Act of Parliament to separate the two funds, with a restriction that the fund formed for one purpose should not be devoted to another. The Government had the good sense to reject such a measure, which, if it had been put into force, would have crippled the powers of unions to relieve their members in times of extraordinary distress.

were taken for the general and gradual extinction of
this feature. Let trade unions have one grand object,
to which the whole of their power and resources can be
devoted, and it will be found that they will succeed
much better by doing that well. By trying too much
they may " botch," if not lose all. " Jack of all trades "
is proverbially " master of none." There is every
reason to believe that unionists are in favour of this
suggestion. The " friendly society " features are seldom
dwelt upon by union advocates. Mr. Dunning does not
include them in his " Philosophy of Trade Unions; " Mr.
W. T. Thornton barely mentions them; the Comte de
Paris says nothing in their favour; and the writers
mentioned in the course of these pages seldom speak of
them. The introduction to the annual reports of trade
unions is the only place where their advantages are
dilated upon. We are there told that the man who
neglects to insure against the "ills that flesh is heir
to " has ever a black shadow before him. "He cannot
tread the earth as independently as other men; for he
knows that, however superior he may be to the frowns
of the world at present, there may come a time when
distress, and possibly beggary, will overtake him."
This is very true and very good, but it is an argument
in favour of a friendly society, not of a trade union.
On the other hand, it must be admitted that benevolent
funds and kindred funds attached to trade unions both
attract members and retain them. In this respect they
are a source of strength, because each man is bound
to obedience under the penalty of losing all the money
he has subscribed for his support in sickness and old
age. Having grown with the growth of the societies,
it would not, perhaps, be wise to interfere in regard to

those already existing. It is, however, worth considering, now that trade unions are legal bodies and have
not to disguise themselves as friendly societies, whether
new organizations that may start should not confine
their operations solely to trade objects.

There are other suggestions which are also worth the
consideration of the executive of trade unions. Some
societies have attempted to limit the amount of work
which each man shall do. This notion, as was shown
in the previous chapter, is not original. It is borrowed
from the Middle Ages. There is nothing positively
wrong in the notion. The men have a perfect right to
do as little work as possible for as much pay as they
can get. It is amusing to notice the high morality with
which masters are suddenly seized when approaching
this portion of the question. They say that such conduct is a wicked and foul conspiracy against the public
welfare. Such conduct, we are told, can only have as
a result scarcity and dearness. It is the aggrandise-
ment of the few at the cost of the many, and one knows
not how many horrors beside. This is all very well,
but the masters must remember that it applies to them
as well as to the men. On the 11th of September, 1874,
the master cotton spinners held a meeting at Manchester, when it was decided " that short time was the
best thing that could be done for the trade." It was
also decided that the following circular should be
addressed to every employer :—" Will you engage to
run four days per week, commencing October 1st, on
condition that all mills working 40,000 spindles engage
to do so ? and if so, will you please say in what way
you would like to work the four days, as the committee
will adopt that mode which the majority of the replies

I

recommend ? " Surely it is now the turn of the men
to be virtuously indignant. In the language of Mr.
Lloyd Jones, parodying the complaint of the masters
on parallel occasions, " the poor strugglers under the
40,000 spindles are not to be consulted. Only the large
men of above 40,000 are worth consideration where a
great *coup* like this is to be made. And what, we ask,
does this modest proposal mean ? In the first instance,
it will take one-third from the wages of the whole of
the workpeople employed in these factories. . . . More
than this—it is a wicked conspiracy against the public
interest. To check production by an arrangement of
this kind means scarcity and dearness ; to diminish production means to increase price ; and to increase price
means simply the taking of money out of the pockets
of the consumers to put it into the capacious pouches
of our manufacturers. What is it to these men if the
worker goes without his wages, or the almost penniless
man without a shirt ? They do not desire to manufacture large quantities at a small profit, but small quantities at a large profit." The fact is, both masters and
men have a perfect right to limit the " out-put." Indeed, at certain seasons such a course would be simply
an act of prudence, and what the unions have to guard
against is the mistake of taking such a step when it is
against the interests of the men to do so.

There are, however, a few of the rules of some trade
unions which are inconsistent with the spirit of the age,
and they ought to be done away with as speedily as
possible. Without at all wishing to insinuate that the
limitation of the number of apprentices is unwise, those
rules which may prevent a father bringing up his son
or sons to his own trade cannot, the author thinks, be

regarded as other than unjust. The attempts, too, to discourage the employment of women and boys are often carried to a ridiculous extreme ; and it was therefore as gratifying to find Mr. Odger and some others of the more intelligent unionists giving their support to the formation of trade unions for women, which in 1874 were being attempted in London and Bristol, as it was pleasing to find that such unions were being established. It may not be out of place here to point out the results of those attempts. None of the unions among women are as yet strong ; still, considering the difficulties to be overcome, their success is remarkable. Women form a class of workers who are very peculiarly situated. In the first place, there is an inherited inclination on their part to rely upon men for assistance and support ; and our existing social system makes them to a great extent dependent upon their male relatives. One of the results of this dependence of women is that the resistance to the downward tendency of their earnings has ever been of the weakest character ; and a similar observation applies to their efforts to reduce the number of working hours. Thus it is that we read of women engaged at trades prejudicial to their health, and working for long hours for the merest pittance. A woman who happens "to be very skilful with the needle, and to have a child old enough and smart enough to give her a little help" may "earn a shilling in a day of twelve hours—a penny an hour!" Attempts have been made to reduce even this rate of wages, which, however, the unions have been able successfully to resist, though only so far as their own members are concerned.

There are no fewer than three millions of women who are earning wages in various industries in England and

Wales, and a few hundreds only are in union. There is, therefore, an ample area for the work that is now going on. A peculiar element in the movement is that there is an organization whose special object is to establish and assist trade unions among women. It is due to Mrs. Paterson that she was the first to hit upon the notion of a Woman's Protective and Provident League which should have for its object the promotion of unionism. With persistent courage and rare ability Mrs. Paterson has, by means of the League, set on foot nineteen unions—ten in London and nine in the provinces. The principal societies are among the bookbinders, the upholsteresses, the shirt and collar-makers, the tailoresses, and the dressmakers, milliners, and mantle-makers. In these unions there are women of all ages from sixteen to seventy, married as well as single, and all the associations are steadily, though not very rapidly, adding to their several reserve funds, and are thus gaining in stability and in efficiency for dealing with some of the evils of overwork and under-payment.

The women's unions, comparatively insignificant as they are at present, can yet show good results. Their influence upon the opinion of men unionists has been very marked. The notion which prompted some of the older unions to prohibit their members from working with women is almost a thing of the past, notwithstanding the recent dispute at Kidderminster on this very question. It is now seen that the interests of labour are best served, not by throwing women out of work with the view of keeping up the wages of men, but by levelling upwards the wages of women, so that if they can do a certain class of work as well as men, they should be paid at the same rate as men. Mr. King, the energetic secretary of the London Consolidated Bookbinders, early saw this, and to his credit did all he could to promote the establishment of the Society of Women Employed in Bookbinding. A similarly liberal spirit soon manifested itself among other trade union secretaries, and it was not long before women delegates were admitted on terms of equality to the Trade Union Congresses. At the last congress seven such delegates attended. Their influence at these gatherings has been great. There are not now, as heretofore, speeches made and resolutions passed against women's work in the various trades, and in 1882 a resolution condemning the employment of mothers in factories and workshops had only one supporter; while at four successive sittings of the congress, from 1878 to 1881, a recommendation that women should be appointed sub-inspectors of factories was unanimously carried.

A strong element of union among women is found in the sympathy and spirit of helpfulness which are characteristic of the sex. These are illustrated in what may be called the subordinate work of the Women's Protective and Provident League. In addition to establishing unions, it has a circulating library, a monthly journal, a savings' bank and co-operative society, an employment register, which prevents women from going to the trouble and fatigue of walking from shop to shop in search of work; a swimming club, a seaside house at Margate, where members can have a bedroom and use of sitting-room for four shillings a week ; and the League by monthly "social meetings" also provides means of recreation and social intercourse which are much appreciated by the members.

There are also some legacies of the dark ages which

ought to—as, indeed, they must *—be swept away. Of course, it is no argument to say that other classes of society have similar silly rules. It may, however, serve to teach some people the wisdom of plucking the beam out of their own eye before they attempt a similar operation on their fellow-men. Lawyers, doctors, and parsons have unions compared to which those of the workmen are insignificant in the amount of dangerous folly they contain in their rules. A "suit" has been adjourned from one term to another—at the cost of the suitors—in order to satisfy the bar etiquette relating to the costume of the counsel. What rule is there in a trade union at all to be compared to that which confines a barrister to a particular circuit, in a country which boasts of free trade? "One," it has been remarked, "has only to watch the progress of an ordinary chancery suit, or to read through an ordinary deed, to find examples which would scarcely lose in lustre by being placed beside some of the brightest examples furnished by the Manchester Bricklayers' Association."

The desire on the part of some unionists not to work with non-unionists is quite a legitimate feeling. Of course there may be differences in opinion as to how far such conduct is gracious or praiseworthy, but that men have the right to refuse to work unless on conditions that suit them no sensible man will deny. They may refuse to work in badly ventilated or unhealthy rooms, or in unsafe mines, with men of known bad character, or, indeed, under any conditions whatever which are disagreeable to them. There must be a strong inclination on the part of unionists not to work

* "They will cure themselves."—W. E. GLADSTONE.

with non-unionists (for reasons stated in the preceding pages) ; and surely if unionists have no right to dictate, they have no call to submit to dictation. Mr. Gladstone, in his speech to the Aston Hall colliers, while acknowledging the right and even the wisdom of action through a union, seems to have forgotten the right of the men to refuse to work with persons against whom they have an antipathy. The present premier told his colliers that " that liberty which the people of this country won for themselves, and have enjoyed for many generations, is the liberty of the few as well as the liberty of the many, and if any workman chooses to work for nothing in the face of a thousand other men, he has as good a right to do so as the thousand have to say what they will work for." It seems strange that a statesman of such acumen as Mr. Gladstone should lay down a doctrine true in every respect, and yet fail to see that it applies to both unionists and non-unionists. If the four non-unionists (which formed the minority to which Mr. Gladstone alluded) have the right to say, "We will work for nothing," surely the thousand unionists have a right to say, "Then we will not work at all." Or reverse the case, and suppose Mr. Gladstone's "minority" became the majority. Let there be one thousand non-unionists and four unionists. Mr. Gladstone would hardly then deny the right of the latter to refuse to work with the former. Of course no general rule can be laid down as to when unionists should work with non-unionists, and when they should refuse to do so. It is in all cases a matter of trade. Mr. Gladstone told the Aston colliers that such a refusal was "mean and dishonourable ; " but far more cogent reasons could be given to show that when society men do work with non-society men, so far as the former are concerned, it is an act of courtesy, if not of commendable charity.

That unions force masters to pay bad workmen the same wages as good workmen is not true, and the very idea would be scouted by all sensible unionists. The notion that such is the case is, however, very general, and it is surprising that Mr. Gladstone himself has fallen into so unpardonable an error. A uniform rate of pay exists in the army, navy, Government offices, and other institutions, in which aristocrats have been able to appropriate the "maximum" of pay, leaving a meagre residuum to their less fortunate brethren; but the trade unionists have not yet learned to practise such injustice. True, the unions sometimes agree upon a minimum rate of wages, but this is quite another thing. If a man be not worth that minimum no employer need engage him, while if he be a man of superior skill, or extraordinary working ability, there is no limit to the amount of wages an employer may feel inclined to give him. Of course, where wages are paid by the day, a uniform rate naturally springs into existence. It is, however, agreed upon between the masters and men. It is a mere conventional arrangement, and may be abandoned by either side as soon as it is found unjust or oppressive. It must be remembered that when wages have settled down to a "uniform rate" that rate is always below the average, and is therefore a gain to the masters. It is a gain to them in another respect, which has been pointed out by Mr. Dunning. So far from placing the competent and incompetent on the same level, says that gentleman, "this 'uniform rate' has been bitterly complained of, as excluding the incompetent altogether. At the Bradford meeting in

1874 one of the speakers gave as a reason against trade unions that he was not able to earn the usual rates, and as the union would not allow any of its members to work for less, he could get no employment while he was a member, and so he left." A "minimum rate" is the rate which the least competent unionist is worth, and if the man cannot come up to that standard the trade society cares not how soon he leaves it. In practice the masters never complain of this "minimum" or "uniform" rate. They know the advantages of it too well to indulge in any such complaint. It is only heard as an argument when they are airing their grievances, and laying the blame of every evil under the sun to the action of trade unions. It is a kind of reasoning which may fairly be considered a special plea.

There are, however, still some traces of a desire amongst unionists to retain rules which would be more honoured in the breach than in the observance—such as the foolish and impolitic regulations which long disgraced the Bricklayers' Society, and which until recently were enforced in all their rigour. The rule that no bricklayer should be allowed to set machine-made bricks could only exist when and where the heads of the bricklayers were as dull as the bricks they set. It requires very little intelligence to discover that the more bricks there are to lay the more bricklayers will be required to lay them; and an extra demand for labour always means a rise in wages. "No bricks to be used in Manchester that are made beyond an arbitrarily fixed boundary line 'averaging about three and a half miles from the Exchange," was the spirit of a rule as absurd and selfish as another which ordered that no bricks should be wheeled in a barrow, or that masters must employ half the men they require resident in Manchester at all their works within fifteen miles of that city; while the existence of a rule that "every bricklayer shall have a labourer to attend upon him, whether there is work for the latter or not," is simply silly. A few such absurdities as these exist in some trade unions, and it would be much better if, being swept away, they were supplanted by the means of promoting technical education, of rules affecting the *quality* of the work, and of any steps which would give a man a better right to the title of " skilled workman " than many of them now possess.*

Perhaps one of the best] means of bringing about such an improvement as that just indicated would be that the utmost possible publicity should be given to the proceedings of trade societies. This would give the public confidence in their decisions, and remove from them the stigma which attaches to them as " secret " societies. There is a current belief that their policy is determined upon in the dark, and carried out in an underhand way. Nothing shakes public confidence so much as the knowledge, or even the idea, that a transaction will not bear the light of day. It is always a suspicious circumstance when public business is conducted privately. Some of the more enlightened societies, it is true, have no objections to the admission of the public to their business meetings, but they take no steps to encourage it. Other societies have, however, begun to be regularly attended by reporters, of which the United Joiners of Glasgow is an instance, while the Operative Bakers, the Saddlers, and many other societies are only too pleased at a

* This is being done. See p. 158.

visit from the representatives of the Press. If it were once known that the eyes of the Press were ever on the societies, the public would feel satisfied and perhaps comfortable. Of course, at times, private matters might be discussed which it would be neither politic nor just should be made public. In such cases the meeting could resolve itself into a committee, when the public and reporters would withdraw. This is the constant practice of town councils, local boards, and school boards; and if it be argued that an arrangement of that kind would enable trade unions to be as secret in the future as it is unjustly thought they have been in the past, it can be replied that no such effect has resulted from the practice amongst the corporations just mentioned. Where there are the greatest facilities given to the Press, as in the House of Commons, there is also the most arbitrary way of excluding reporters, and how seldom that power is exercised is well known.

It remains to recommend the unionists to keep from the appearance of evil. Stress has been laid upon the difficult and delicate task the general secretary has to perform. He has to work, too, beneath the searching eye of a bitter enemy who is ever ready to pounce upon the simplest act of indiscretion and magnify it to a crime. He is an object of envy and jealousy to those even who have elected him to the post, and even his mannerisms are charged against him as faults. I knew one secretary described as "caddish" because on a particular occasion he placed a handkerchief on his head to protect his neuralgia from a cold wind. Of course to the impartial inquirer wheat is easily distinguishable from chaff, but it is as well that partial inquirers should have as little to lay hold of as possible. Perhaps the

day has gone when delegates "will relate exultingly
how, at Stockport, after persuading a set of operatives
to turn out, they arranged with the masters, for a consideration, to get them to turn in again; how at Bolton
they got 50s. a head for persuading some factory hands
on strike to go back to work on the same terms as
before." Perhaps, too, we shall hear no more of delegates who, for sixteen weeks, did nothing but "sup
ale;" or of that class of man who, speaking of the
Preston strike, said, "and, by God, I don't mean 'em to
go in again as long as they gie me my two guineas a
week and my travelling expenses." All this is passing
away. Here, however, is not the place to moralize. It
is well known that the men are no bigger saints than
their masters. Society, however, winks at the faults of
broadcloth, but is horrified at the mistakes of fustian.
It was doubtless very indiscreet on the part of Mr.
Halliday and his friends when, during the South Wales
strike in 1872, they refused the offer of the masters that
an auditor appointed by the men should inspect their
books, so that the justice or injustice of the men's demand
might be demonstrated. Of course, the masters knew
their own position, and could fearlessly offer to submit it
to the scrutiny. It is well known what charges were
bandied about after this refusal; and the *Financial
Reformer*, which pretends to be the working man's
friend *par excellence*, did not hesitate to charge Mr.
Halliday with "fomenting and keeping alive" the dispute for personal motives. So also it is sometimes
widely and somewhat authoritatively asserted that some
of the officers of the Agricultural Labourers' Union
kept alive the recent dispute from interested motives.
There are some persons whose only logic consists in the

proverb that wherever there is smoke there must be a fire, and it would therefore be well to take care that there is as little smoke as possible upon which such persons can reason.

It has been shown, 1st, That trade unions are the natural growth of natural laws, and that their development has been marvellously rapid; 2nd, That their faults (now diminishing) are not inherent or essential, but are either excrescences or mere copies from other corporations; 3rd, That the object of unionism is a legitimate and a noble one; and 4th, That their fitness to attain that object is abundantly proved by the brilliant success which has characterized their efforts. It remains to consider what has been the influence of that success, to which task the following chapter will be devoted.

CHAPTER V.

TRADE UNIONS—THEIR INFLUENCE.

Effects of high wages—Desire to retain a high social standard—
Well-paid labour remunerative to the capitalist—Foreign
competition—High wages does not mean high prices—The
high price of coal and the colliers—Socialism—Co-operation—
Trade unions stimulate invention—Expenditure by the working classes—Advantages of shorter hours—Self-improvement
—Moral influence of trade unions—Endeavour to make good
workmen—Educational influences of trade unions—Political
influence—Future of trade unions—Legal requirements—Class
distinctions—Good conduct of unionists insisted upon—
Mutual assistance—The union offices storehouses of statistics
—The British Association on trade unions—Recapitulation
and conclusion.

IT remains to consider—

    (a) What is the influence of trade unions on the
    trade of the country?

    (b) What is their moral effect on those who belong
    to them?

We are met at the outset with the assertion that the
principle of trade unionism is as much the principle of
monopoly as was that of the guilds of the Middle Ages.
The trade societies, it is said, have a sort of "protective"
influence, using the word in contradistinction to "free
trade," now the acknowledged custom of the country.

Of all places in the world it is astonishing to find that this doctrine was, ten years ago, diligently promulgated in the publications of the Financial Reform Association, an association established in 1848 to advocate "perfect freedom of trade." It is gratifying to find, however, that although the dogma was repeated page after page with tedious iteration, yet no argument was adduced in support of it. Of abuse, however, there was abundance, and one soon sees that, after all, the Liverpool financial reformers were willing to give free trade to the rich capitalist, but they would deny it to the poor labourer. It is, however, very doubtful whether the then executory of the association knew what trade unionism really is. They seemed to have taken all their notions of unionists and unionism from newspaper paragraphs about Broadhead ; and, indulging in a vast amount of rhodomontade, they did scruple to draw upon imagination for facts, and to so far forget the rules of courtesy and good behaviour as to insult those of their own officers even who ventured to upbraid them. The hatred of the association to unionism was only surpassed by its horror of and vindictiveness towards unionists. Surely they must have exclaimed with Hobbie Elliott's grandmother, " Oh, if there was the law, and the douce, quiet administration of justice that makes a kingdom flourish in righteousness, the like o' them suldna be suffered to live !" Trade unionists are all, we were told, " either knaves or fools." Their true prototype, said these charitable men, is found in the "*black* slave-driver," who, we were reminded, was proverbially the most cruel and ferocious of any.*

* It is proper to say that when Mr. Edmund Knowles Muspratt, a very clear-headed and liberal politician, who would be a great

There is, however, a redeeming point in all this. Although ruffianism had taken the place of argument, and blackguardism had been found where logic was expected —although the trade union leaders were called "Sheffield Thugs," and their followers "fools," yet it seemed that, after all, such strong language was only a coarse way of saying that the sole fault of unionism was the ignorance or inability of unionists. At least, that is all that can be made out of the one sentence of common sense buried in paragraph after paragraph, and page after page, of folly, abuse, and untruth. It is once, and only once, confessed that "if trade unionists knew how to state their own case properly, they would be invincible."

It would hardly have been worth while mentioning the above were it not for the fact, not only that the association referred to claims to be the supreme authority in matters of free trade, but it is an association supported chiefly by working men; and it is especially careful to circulate its publications amongst the artisan class. There are, however, others who hold the same doctrine, and it is quite proper, therefore, that it should be refuted here. The answer may be given in a few words. Have persons a right to withhold a commodity from the market in order to raise its price ? Is such a proceeding a violation of the principles of free trade ? If the cotton brokers of Liverpool hold back their stocks in the hope of forcing an advance in price, the financial reformers in that town will hardly have the fortitude to ask that they should be obliged to sell. Free trade must be free to the buyer as well as the seller, and to

acquisition to the House of Commons, was elected president of the Financial Reform Association in 1874, he ordered the executory to desist from its insane and ungentlemanly behaviour, the seller as well as the buyer. The cotton brokers may—nay, do—keep back their cotton in order to enhance its price. The labourers combine and say : "We want so much for our labour, which we know is useful to you, and unless you give us that price we will forego a certain quantity of our labour—we will waste it, in fact—in the hope that you will be obliged to yield, which in the end will be a benefit to us." It is to be hoped that the Financial Reform Association have intelligence enough to see that there is as much justice in the one case as in the other. It is, indeed, the " higgling of the market," as Adam Smith calls it ; and those who do not "higgle," even when " shopping," will generally pay more than the market rate for their goods. Strikes, then, are not only legitimate, but they are the inevitable result of commercial bargaining for labour. They are no more opposed to free trade than are lockouts. If a man may say to his men, or to a portion of them, "Business is slack, I give you a week's notice," surely when the state of trade is reversed the men may say, " Trade is brisk, give us more wages, or take a week's notice." "I do not hesitate to say," says one who is worth hearing,* " that the associations of labourers, of a nature similar to trade unions, far from being a hindrance to a free market for labour, are the necessary instrumentality of that free market—the indispensable means of enabling the sellers of labour to take due care of their own interests under a system of competition." Indeed, the whole question is so axiomatic, that had not the position been raised elsewhere, no mention of it would have been made here. It seems strange that persons can be found who will deny that all legal means

* Mr. J. S. Mill.

K

employed by those who live by labour to increase the remuneration for that labour, or to shorten the hours of labour—which amounts to the same thing—or to render their means of living more secure, are no more a violation of the principles of free trade than is the conduct of a dealer who withholds his goods from the market in order to raise their price.

It has been shown in the previous chapter that one of the great results of trade unionism has been to raise wages, and under this head, therefore, it is a no less important inquiry—What are the effects of advanced wages on the trade of the country? Now, high wages —*i.e.* not only a greater number of shillings a week, but no-diminution in their purchasing power—cannot be otherwise than a great blessing. A great deal has been said on the wasteful way in which the extra earnings of the working men were squandered in 1873 and the year before, and this will be treated of in the sequel. All a man's extra earnings, however, were not wasted. Some portion of them was, doubtless, spent in sober gratification, and in increasing the comfort of the household. Now one of the articles in which there has been increased consumption is tea. Let us ask, therefore, what is the effect of an increased consumption of tea? It signifies, in the first place, that more ships have been required to fetch the tea from China, to build which ships more men were required, and to man them more men were wanted. The ships had to be rigged, which was good for the ropemakers and the sailcloth manufacturers, as well as several other industries. Then when the tea arrived here, it required more warehouses and employed more warehousemen, as well as an additional number of carriers, both by rail and road, to distribute it over the country; it required more paper to wrap it in parcels, more string to tie them with Indeed, it is difficult to imagine any industry whatever that does not receive some advantage from the increase in the consumption of any single article; and it may be a consolation to cosmopolitans to be reminded that the processes here alluded to are not confined in their advantages to this country, but stimulate in a similar way the various trades in the distant land which cultivated the plant; and thus two nations mutually benefit each other, and feel that they have an interest in each other's prosperity. This, however, is not all. The tea is not sent here for nothing; we send out other commodities in exchange for it. The cotton fabrics from Lancashire, the woollen cloths from Yorkshire, hardware goods from Birmingham, and steel and iron manufactures from Sheffield, are gathered to our ports and sent to the east, employing labour at every process, and whenever they are moved, from the time the raw material is landed on our shores until the time that it is delivered over to the consumer or the wearer in a far distant land. When the collier's wife buys an alpaca dress she little thinks how much the world has been set in motion to enable her to do so—how that Salt wove it, Ripley dyed it, Lairds built the ship to fetch it, Whitworths made the tools in order that Platt might make the machines, in order that it might be spun, woven, dyed, pressed, before it reached the dressmaker, who used a needle made by Milward, and thread by Brooks. An increase in the consumption of a commodity, therefore, gives work to thousands who would be otherwise idle, and has a tendency to raise wages nearer and nearer to the "just rate," which has ever been such a bone of contention. This is the great point to remember—when men are earning money they spend it. They buy more furniture for their homes, more clothes for their back, more beer for their cellar, more and better food. It is only when wages are low that, like Christopher Sly, they have "no more doubtlets than backs, no more stockings than legs, nor no more shoes than feet." The prosperity of the working man, then, increases the prosperity of the butcher, the baker, the publican, the grocer, the tailor, the draper, and all the manufactures and industries upon which these trades depend. It may, indeed, be the prosperity of the nation which causes high wages; but it is equally certain that high wages maintain and increase that prosperity. *

The working men, having once tasted the sweets of a prosperous condition, do not like to return to their old ways of poverty and squalor. They are always found, therefore, struggling to maintain their wages at the maximum point they have ever reached. The reluctance which is now (1884) being shown to submit to a necessary reduction is evidence in proof of this. Now it has been shown by Ricardo, Mill, and others, that the minimum rate of wages is found amongst men in that condition below which they do not choose to live. If these men can be improved in their condition, and when that "improvement is of a signal character, and a generation grows up which has always been used to an improved scale of comfort, the habits of this new gene-

* The shopkeepers know this, and often assist to maintain a strike by giving the men credit while they were out of work. Experience has taught them that when men have high wages they spend them, and they therefore assist the men to obtain an advance, knowing that they themselves will share the benefits.

ration, in respect to population, become formed upon
a higher minimum, and the improvement in their condition becomes permanent." Here, then, is an object
worth striving for—a "permanent" raising of wages
—at any rate so permanent that it will not fall for
one generation—truly a consummation devoutly to be
wished, and one which may be reached, not only without
injury to the capitalist, but to his material prosperity
and advantage. On the other hand, a permanent fall
in wages means a deterioration in the "minimum"
condition. When men begin to fall, they descend more
rapidly than they rise, and in a few weeks will forget
the comforts they enjoyed for a few months. *Facilis
decensus Averno.* There can be no doubt that it was
this "keeping down" in years gone by that permanently injured the condition of the agricultural
labourers, from which injury they are only now re-
covering. There can be no higher mission for trade
unions than that of raising the condition of the working
men of this country to such an extent and for such a
length of time that the point reached becomes the
accepted minimum, and that any change at all must
be in an upward direction.

The labourers, however, must not expect to derive all
the advantages of high wages at once. They must
remember that if enhanced wages cause the price of
the commodity produced to be enhanced, the price is
raised to them as well as to others. If the demand of
the cotton operatives raise the price of shirts, the
cotton operatives must pay more for their shirts just
the same as other people. There is, however, this
to be considered, that men produce faster than they
consume. Each man produces more than is necessary

for his own support.   When a man has made a plough
he can make another before that one is worn out.   The
more there are made the more there will be wanted until
all are supplied, which for practical purposes may at
present be considered a very remote future.   The supply
creates the demand.   Stockings were not inquired for
(because they were not wanted) until they were invented ; and if to-morrow we had double the quantity
we have to-day, it might be possible to sell them at half
the present price without reducing wages at all.   It is
quite possible that wages may be enhanced, prices
diminished, and profits increased, at one and the same
time, as those familiar with the use of newly invented
machinery are well aware.   This explains a paradoxical
appearance at the present day, viz. that all over the
world there is a tendency of wages to rise, and at the
same time a universal tendency of all materials to
cheapen.   Unionism helps both those tendencies, and is
thus a double blessing.   It is probable, though not
certain, that profits will be called upon to make the
principal sacrifice in the future.   At any rate this is to
be hoped.   Hitherto the consumer has been—to use a
vulgar but expressive word—fleeced ; and it is time
that the incidence of injustice be either shifted or
annihilated.

Although, however, a rise in the price of labour all
round taxes, so to speak, the labourers themselves, yet
it does not tax them to the full extent of the advance.
There is a race of beings called "non-producers"—a
class "sometimes innocent, generally useless, often
noxious."   Now a rise in wages all round means that
some of the luxuries of the non-producing class are
being metamorphosed into extra comforts or luxuries

for the producing class. This is a pure gain to the producer, in addition to other gains which result from the improvement of his position. The only way by which labourers could be deprived of the benefits of increased wages would be by the non-labouring class setting to work and producing something. They would then share in the advantages of the increased prosperity, instead of, as now, sacrificing a portion of their means, and this portion is divided amongst the producers. So long, however, as they toil not, neither do they spin, and garner what they have not gathered, they cannot complain that they contribute towards the cost of those who work.

It must not be thought, however, that well-paid labour is unremunerative to the capitalist. The contrary is the fact. Indeed, that style of labour for which no wages—in the ordinary sense—are paid, is the least remunerative of any. Slaves will not work. The low state of civilization and the ignorance of even the simplest laws in which it is found necessary to keep human beings, in order that they may submit to slavery, do more to prevent them from working hard than the lash does to make them work at all. It was pointed out some time ago that "two Middlesex mowers will mow in a day as much grass as six Russian serfs; and in spite of the dearness of provisions in England, and their cheapness in Russia, the mowing of a quantity of hay which would cost an English farmer a copeck will cost a Russian proprietor three or four copecks." It was, in short, considered as proven that in Russia, where everything was cheap, the labour of a serf was doubly as expensive as that of a labourer in England. Men will not work their very best unless they have an incentive to do so. This great truth has at last made itself known to some of our great capitalists. Sir Thomas Brassey and other large employers have found out that underpaid labour is by no means economical. Here are a few proofs—When the North Devon Railway was being made, men were working at 2s. a day at first, then 2s. 6d., and then 3s. 6d. Nevertheless it was found that the work was executed more cheaply at the highest rate than at the lowest rate. So also in carrying out the large sewage works in Oxford-street, London, brick-layers were gradually raised from 6s. to 10s. a day, and at the higher rate of wages bricks were laid at a cheaper rate ; while at the building of Basingstoke Station one London workman at 5s. 6d. a day did more work than three country ones at 3s. 6d. each. Many other instances might be added, all showing that intelligent workmen well paid are cheaper than bad workmen ill paid. As Mr. Frederic Harrison puts it : " The workman whose intelligence requires no more than the minimum of supervision is a cheap bargain even at the maximum wages." " It is said by one of our factory inspectors that in France one workman looks after 14 spindles. In England one minder and two assistants can manage a mule with 2200 spindles. It is an obvious economy to employ such a minder at even higher rates as compared with the French. This is the process by which, in our cotton industry, as in so many others, wages have been rising, profits have been growing, and goods have been cheapened all at the same time." Increased wages are always to be got when there is an increase in the product of labour, although even the rate of wages be lower. Thus a spinner in Glasgow (Messrs. Houldsworth's) employed on a mule, and spinning cotton 120 hanks to the pound, produced in 1823, working 74½ hours in the week, 46 pounds of yarn, his nett weekly earnings for which amounted to 26s. 7d. In 1833, the rate of wages having in the meantime been reduced 13½ per cent., and the time of working having been lessened to 69 hours, the spinner was enabled, by the greater perfection of the machinery, to produce on a mule of the same number of spindles, 52½ pounds of yarn of the same fineness, and his nett weekly earnings advanced to 29s. 10d. Similar causes raised the remuneration of the fast spinners from 5s. 6d. a week in 1871 by successive gradations to 9s. in 1872; and almost every trade can tell the same story. Sir Thomas Brassey strengthens this position by pointing out that in the construction of the Paris and Rouen Railway, although the English navvies earned 5s. a day, while the Frenchmen employed received only 2s. 6d. a day, yet it was found, on comparing the cost of two adjacent cuttings in precisely similar circumstances, that the excavation was made at a lower cost per cubic yard by the English navvies than by the French labourers; and it must be remembered, too, that the former worked one and a half hours a day less than the latter. Another authority has told us that, a few years ago, ten labourers in Ireland raised the same quantity of produce that four labourers raised in England, and the result of the work of the one was generally inferior in quality to that of the other. Quarry-owners tell the same tale, and it was the opinion of the late Sir Francis Crossley that our agricultural labourers would do more work if they were better paid.

Although, therefore, wages increase, labour does not become dearer. This is very gratifying, because it can

hardly be doubted that the spread of education, and the
comforts which follow from it, will induce the working
man to work less hard, and for shorter time, for increased wages, than he has hitherto done.   The facts
above stated, too, should serve to lay that frightful
hobgoblin—"foreign competition."   A ship can hardly
be launched in America, or a furnace lighted in Belgium
but England is assured that in consequence of strikes
the trade is leaving the country.   The most trade will
always be found where there are the best workmen, and
the argument of these pages shows how these are to be
made.   It is very amusing to notice that while British
capitalists pretend to be alarmed at foreign competition,
every nation under the sun is afraid of English competition.   When our cotton manufacturers were earning 12s. to 15s. a week, those in France, Belgium, and
Germany were earning 7s. 3d. to 9s. 7d., and those in
Russia were content with 2s. 4d. to 2s. 11d.; and yet
the one thing dreaded by the continental nations
mentioned was actually the competition of the British.
Such fears on the part of a thickly populated country
like England are groundless in the face of the scarcity
of labour in some countries, and its entire absence from
others.   The facility with which people jump to conclusions is something extraordinary.   Concurrent facts
are too often accepted as causes.   The public are
generally too ready to accept the "invariable antece-
dent" as a cause; and when a few cargoes of Swedish
ore are imported into England, after a dispute in the
iron trade, the newspapers gravely tell us that trade
unionism is ruining the country, while a little inquiry
would have told them that the one was probably no
more caused by the other than that the railway collision

at Wigan was due to the burning cigars which Mr.
Spurgeon nightly smokes to the "glory of God." The
story is, indeed, an old one, and its constant recital is
tedious. It was heard as long ago as 1828, when it was
stated that in consequence of a "strong union" in
Dublin, the shipbuilding trade on the banks of the
Liffey were destroyed. A little inquiry would have
satisfied an impartial judge that, as vessels in Dublin
then cost £3 5s. 6d. per ton for repairs alone, while in
Liverpool, Sunderland, and other places, the same class
of vessels could be bought out-and-out for £1. 10s. per
ton, there was ample reason why the trade should leave
the Liffey; and as in the towns to which the trade was
attracted there were also "strong unions," it is little
less than an Irish bull to take the view which was
taken by the Dublin shipbuilders. In June, 1874, a
correspondent in the *Times* used as an argument against
trade unionism, that it had driven the shipbuilding
trade away from the Thames. When so much careless-
ness is displayed in attempts to ascertain the truth, and
when such rash conclusions are drawn from false
premises, what is alone proved is the obtuseness of the
writer. Unions exist on the banks of the Tyne, the
Mersey, the Umber, the Clyde, and elsewhere. If,
therefore, the result of unionism be to drive away the
shipbuilding trade, how is it that it affects the Thames
alone? If the writer in the *Times* had taken the
trouble—as he ought to have done—to inquire into the
cost of shipbuilding on the banks of the Thames, where
there is no iron or coal, and compared that cost with
the expense of building ships on the banks of rivers
near which there is an abundance of both coal and
iron, he would have found that the same causes which

destroyed the shipbuilding trade in the Liffey also drove the trade from the Thames to the Tyne.

Professor Cairns, a careful and thoughtful economist, admits that it is often better to employ good workmen at high wages than to employ bad workmen at low wages. It is strange, however, that in another argument the Professor overlooks that admission. He places the power of a trade union at a lower point than any other economist who has given them a word of praise. He states that all a union can do is to enforce a rise when it should take place—and not always then; but he thinks them incompetent to obtain a rise when the economic conditions do not warrant a rise. Surely Professor Cairns misunderstands the object of a trade union, if he think a part of its programme is to attempt to obtain a rise when economic conditions do not warrant such rise. Failure would be certain to follow such a policy. The differences between employers and employed do not arise from any such notion, but from the general policy of the masters in systematically refusing to acknowledge that the economic conditions are ever such as to warrant a rise. As Professor Cairns says, the question is : " Is there a margin of wealth which workmen by combination can conquer ? " The men think there is not a mere margin, but a vast territory to which they are entitled, and the experiences of the past fill them with sure and certain hopes as to the future. They see the final result, and are determined upon its speedy realization. Nor do they fear that which Professor Cairns dreads, viz. that in consequence of advanced wages, capital must be withdrawn, and wages therefore fall. Such can only be the case when wages are *unduly* advanced, about which there need be no alarm. At any rate, the workmen have no such fear. They are alive to the admission made by Professor Cairns, to which allusion has been made; and they are acquainted with the facts above given, showing that well-paid, intelligent artisans, when not overworked, are always cheapest in the end.

It may be mentioned here, in parenthesis, that although trade unions have a far more powerful influence over wages—constantly imparting an upward tendency — than Professor Cairns imagines, yet it is likewise an error on the part of those who think that trade unionism seeks to determine the rate of wages. It cannot do that; it cannot do more than affect them. A trade society may retard a fall or accelerate a rise, but it cannot change the law which regulates the fluctuations, or render permanent that which in its very essence is temporary.

It is at once seen that the instances of well-paid but remunerative labour, added to those facts which were adduced in support of a similar argument in the previous chapter in regard to the reduction of the hours of labour, show that the beneficial effects of the success of unionism on the trade of the country are not at the cost of the capitalist, but to his advantage, and that that advantage is not less but greater by his paying higher wages for shorter hours.

This is in contradiction of those widespread assertions that prices must be increased because wages have been raised. A notable instance of the promulgation of this falsehood is found in connection with the famine prices demanded for coal in 1873. There is an old saying to the effect that persons of a certain class should be blessed with good memories; and it would have been

as well if the coalowners had remembered that, so far
from the increase of wages causing a rise in the price
of coal, the latter took place before the first was heard
of. The increase in the rate of wages followed, and did
not precede, the rise in the price of coal; and it is yet to
be learnt that the effect precedes the cause. It is now
seen that coal rose in price from natural causes. There
was, first, the demand for iron from Germany at the
close of the war; second, the vast extension of railways
throughout the world, especially in America; and third,
the increase in iron shipping, other manufactures being
at the same time in a prosperous condition. A large
amount of capital, also, had accumulated in 1871, and
investors in chemical works, in manufactories of textile
fabrics, etc., drew cheques, as Earl Fitzwilliam put
it, upon the bank of our coalfields. The men, who had·
succeeded in obtaining a Mines Regulation Act, took
advantage of a natural advance of price to ask for a
natural increase of wages, upon which the masters,
instead of at once conceding, delayed until they were
obliged to yield; and they then, by combined action,
ran up coal to famine prices, ignored the causes just
mentioned, and threw the blame upon the working of
of the Mines Regulation Act, and the demands of the
men.

The claims of the men to a signal advance of wages
were very great—their demands extremely moderate.
When, for instance, the cost of getting coal increased
from 60 to 65 per cent., but the selling price had
increased 120 per cent., it would, indeed, have been
extraordinary if the workmen had not pressed for
higher wages. In Cumberland, from December, 1871,
to January, 1874, wages had increased 56 per cent., and

the price of coal 145 per cent. In the Barnsley district, when the masters were getting an increased profit of 6s. a ton, it was with great difficulty that the men could wring from that profit an increase of 8d. a ton as their share.* When the South Staffordshire and East Worcestershire coalmasters met the demand of the men for one shilling a day increase by a concession of six-pence, they, on the very same day, raised the price of coal 2s. a ton. In 1871 coke was worth, at the pits in the Durham coalfield, about 9s. to 10s. 6d. per ton. In 1873 it had risen to a forced value of from 37s. 6d. to 42s. 6d. a ton, or more than 400 per cent. ! Coal worth from 5s. 6d. to 7s. 6d. per ton for the best quality at the pit in 1871, had risen in 1873 to something like 20s. to 25s., an advance of about 350 per cent. Now, we have heard on all hands of the rapacity of the colliers, and yet the advance in their wages—not obtained without extreme pressure being put on the colliery owners—did not reach an average of 100 per cent. at the outside. In short, it may be taken as conceding a great deal to an opponent when it is stated that, speaking generally, when coal advanced from 7s. 5d. to 15s. a ton, only from 1s. 6d. to 3s. a ton of that advance were for wages, and even so much would not have been obtained but for the action of the unions. Where, then, is the ground for the pretence that the large demands of the miners were amongst the main causes of the high price of coal ? The profits have gone to the masters, who

---

* "It is not the strikes or the trade unions which have raised the price of coal. A large coalowner has told me that the price of coal, within the last twelve months, has increased 15s. a ton, while the rate of colliers' wages has increased only 1s. 6d. a ton." —Sir Wm. Harcourt, in the House of Commons, 6th June, 1873.

have a strong combination amongst themselves, the practical result of which, by fixing the selling price of coal, is to force the consumer to pay not only all the naturally enhanced price of coal, but a sensational or "panic" price as well. Yet, strange to relate, the complaint against that combination was very feeble and far from general. It is indeed surprising that when the public—or a portion of them—combine as co-operators, so that the tradesmen shall not get too large a profit, no one complains but the shopkeepers; that when capitalists combine to obtain enormous profits at the cost of everybody, nobody grumbles; and it is not until the workmen combine, in order to get increased wages for their labour, that all the world is alarmed, and cries out in despair that the country is going to pieces.

To show the extent to which a masters' combination exerts its power, the following incident is related, the names of the parties concerned being for obvious reasons suppressed. In Liverpool, not long ago, a coal merchant with extensive connections advertised his intention to reduce the price of house coal by 2s. per ton, on and after a certain date. In forming that resolution, however, he seems to have reckoned entirely "without his host"; for no sooner had the advertisement appeared than he received notice from two extensive colliery proprietors that they would stop his supplies in the winter if he did anything of the kind. So, under pressure from coalowners, he had to withdraw his advertisement, and to continue to charge his customers 2s. per ton more than he considered a fair profit on his transactions. Surely it is the masters and not the men who keep the coal *down* in the earth and *up* in the price.

It was very surprising to notice the facility with which the masters, in 1874, forced a general reduction of wages. Even if the fall in price demanded such a reduction—which is by no means clear—yet it is strange that the men so readily *believed* their employers. Great care is taken to register the prices of all commodities; very little attention is bestowed to registering the rates of wages. It is, I think, Mr. Frederic Harrison who points out that even newspapers, speaking of commodities, announce an "upward tendency," or a "slight improvement," or "an increased buoyancy;" but that no such steps are taken in regard to labour. On the other hand, "one of the most experienced engineers in England, the secretary of one of our most useful com-missions, has repeatedly said that he never knew a labour question in which employers published the truth." The inconsistency of the masters, too, is often very startling. Thus when the West Yorkshire colliers demanded an increase of wages, because the price of coal had advanced, the reply of the owners was that the price of coal had nothing whatever to do with the rate of wages. No sooner, however, did coal fall than the owners demanded a reduction of wages, stating that although "the price of coal did not directly control the ratio of the rate of wages, yet they could not conceal from themselves that it had some effect, and that it was, at any rate, an index of the time when a rise or fall in wages should take place." It is a pity they did not see this when an increase was demanded! When, too, the men have asked for an advance of, say, 10 per cent., and the masters have not only refused it, but, as has often taken place, demanded a reduction of 10 per cent. out of sheer opposition, it is indeed surprising that

L

the men have shown so much forbearance. With some few exceptions, the men have asked for "Peace on fair terms;" and the masters have answered, "War, and an unconditional surrender." The men have asked for bread, and have received a stone. One of the best influences that trade unionism can have on the trade of the country is the one which teaches the masters that what is sought is not a favour, but justice; and that as the manufacturer makes as much as he can out of the dealer, so will the weaver make as much as he can out of the manufacturer. The sooner the masters see this the better. Professor Fawcett says "there must constantly be a deadening influence depressing industry as long as antagonism of interest continues between employers and employed, and the noblest, highest, and in every sense best efforts of trade unionism are those that tend to remove that antagonism."

There can, indeed, be little doubt that the unions have made many a great and praiseworthy sacrifice in submitting to reductions. In order to avoid a collision the men have yielded their just rights with very little grumbling. It by no means follows that because coal falls in price that wages must immediately fall. In order to justify a fall in wages it is necessary that the price of coal (or, of course, any other commodity that may be under consideration) should fall below that point at which an advance took place. The men have a right to resist any attempt to reduce wages until such a state of affairs comes about. Now, according to the Coal Committee, the average price of six qualities of coal at the Manston Collieries, in West Yorkshire, at the pit's mouth, was, in 1871, 5s. 8d.; in 1872, 9s. 3d.; in 1873, 13s. 1d. The price at Pease's Adelaide Colliery, in Durham, was 7s. 5d. in 1870 ; 13s. 6d. in 1872; and 15s. in 1873. These prices were for all qualities of coal. The highest price of coke for the iron trade, put in trucks at the oven at Pease's West Collieries, in Durham, was, in 1870, 12s. 6d. ; in 1873, 42s. 6d. In addition, coal which was practically unsaleable before, and thrown aside in immense heaps as mere rubbish, found a brisk demand at from 7s. 6d. to 12s. 6d. per ton. Now, it would be certainly unfair, when coal had gone up from 9s. 3d. to 13s. 1d. before wages were increased, to expect the men to submit to a return to the old amount because the price of coal falls to 10s. When the price of coal has advanced 400 per cent. it can hardly be expected, if coals fall only 200 per cent., that the men will obey the command, "As you were." In some parts of England—as in the cotton districts and elsewhere—this has evidently presented itself to the minds of the union leaders, and causes strikes to be threatened.

It is sometimes said, in reply to the above argument, that the price of a commodity is not a proper basis upon which to settle the rate of wages. The proper basis it is said, is the cost of production, upon which basis a minimum (of say 5 per cent.) and a maximum (of say 12½ per cent.) can be fixed upon. It would be out of place to argue here on the proper principle by which wages should be regulated or determined. Indeed, it seems to be a matter of taste more than anything else. In an award given by Mr. Joseph Chamberlain, who arbitrated in the South Staffordshire dispute, the price of coal was agreed upon as the basis ; but that is no reason why the West Yorkshire owners and workers should not select "cost of production" if they wish, though, as "wages" must always be an item in the price of production, it renders the standard more unstable. The question is really one for the boards of arbitration, or for agreements between masters and men. What is pertinent to the matter under consideration is this : that, whichever standard be selected, there should be a sufficient fall in the prices of commodities which have risen rapidly to justify a serious fall in the rate of wages. In 1874 the price of coal for iron manufacturing purposes was quoted at a reduction to 12s. 6d. Now, on the best authority it can be stated that when wages were at their highest and coal was at the highest, the "cost of production" was not more than 7s. a ton at the pit's mouth, giving the masters a profit of 8s. A fall of 3s. or 4s. a ton, therefore, was hardly a reason why wages should be greatly reduced, if even (which is very questionable) it justified any reduction at all.

Professor Fawcett pointed out some years ago that the tendency to make a rise of wages in any particular trade usually consequent upon a rise of profits was a commencement of that regular participation of the labourers in the profits derived from their labour, which would ultimately develop into what is known as "co-operation." Mr. J. S. Mill, Mr. W. T. Thornton, and a host of others, amongst them even some prominent trade unionists, have argued in the same strain. It may be a sign of stupidity, if not an evidence of presumption and even impudence, on the part of the author, when he confesses that he is obliged to disagree with such great and powerful authorities. There does not present itself to his mind any evidence that such a goal is before us, or that, if so, it would be desirable to reach it; and he can only express his belief that it is a pretty fancy, which perhaps can hardly be more prettily expressed than in the graceful and elegant poem which Mr. Thornton has introduced in his book "On Labour." It is all very well to stand "in spirit upon Pisgah's brow," and with "prescient rapture" view—what? Why, a world of humdrum sameness. Imagine a people without leaders, working like a clock, but with no one possessed of power to wind it up. Surely it would come to a standstill. Mr. Thornton fails to point out the incentive for any one of his Utopians to do any manner of work. In fact, he eliminates the incentive.

> "Brethren, unjostled by the envious press
>   Of all competitious rivalry, for all
> Shared equally, none coveting excess,
>   Each in such office laboured as might fall
> To him most fitly,—such as several taste
>   Or special talent made congenial:
>
>   *   *   *   *   *
>
>   . . . . and his gathering brought,
> And at the commonweal's disposal placed:
>   Nor larger meed for larger service sought;
> Who gathered much had nothing over, nor
>   To him who gathered little lacked there aught,
> Weakly or strong, with equal effort bore
>   Each one his due proportion, nor did they
> Who added largelier to the general store
>   More merit therefore claim, nor aught betray
> Save gratitude for ampler strength bestowed,
>   Wherewith an ampler measure to purvey."

It seems, then, that in labour's Utopia the reward for industry, diligence, strength, ability, talent, and general superiority is to be—gratitude. There could hardly be a stronger incentive to idleness: there could not be a better plan suggested to prevent invention, to emasculate one's faculties, and to rob life of almost all its pleasures. Where would be the stimulus which creates genius? That individuality which, as Mr. Mill points out, is one of the elements of well-being, without which, indeed, he says, the progressive career of a people ceases, would be sought for in vain; and there would only be found dull and blunt natures. The principle being based on "equality," the mind itself would bow to the yoke. There would be no great men, and "it is really important not only what men do, but also what manner of men they are that do it. . . . Human nature is not a machine to be built after a model, and set to do exactly the work prescribed for it, but a tree, which requires to grow and develop itself on all sides, according to the tendency of the inward forces which make it a living thing." There would, in a purely co-operative state of society, be no struggle, no desire on the part of men to make a choice of anything, and the "human faculties of perception, judgment, discriminative feeling, mental activity, and even moral preference, are exercised only in making a choice." To eat as much as possible and work as little as possible would be the natural result of a state of society in which gratitude is the only wages, and in which even that wages is dealt out alike to the feeble and idle, as well as to those who have borne the heat and burden of the day. Capital possessed by an individual would be "accumulated shame;" and if a man were found to have accumulated ever so little, he would be spurned as "false to his fellow-men," while he who attempted to secure a comfortable independence would be regarded with horror and repugnance. The Utopia pointed out by M.

Comte, and to which trade unionism in many respects tends, is far more likely to be realized. That great French philosopher and reformer points out that mankind, having to act together, are necessarily "organized and classed with some reference to their unequal aptitudes, natural or acquired, which demand that some should be under the direction of others, scrupulous regard being at the same time had to the fulfilment towards all of the claims rightfully inherent in the dignity of a human being; the aggregate of which, still very insufficiently appreciated, will constitute more and more the principle of universal morality as applied to daily use." Trade unions are particularly fitted to inculcate such principles as these; while the self-sacrificing ἰδέα which pervades the rules of most trade societies, and to which attention will be directed in the course of the following pages, is an excellent means of preparing men's minds for the doctrine that it is their duty to restrain the pursuit of personal objects when that pursuit is of no benefit to others; and ultimately a state of morality so high may be reached that men will feel themselves called upon to sacrifice even innocent indulgences for the benefit of their fellow-men. "Love thy neighbour as thyself" was an excellent command, now superseded by "Love thy neighbour *better* than thyself."

When the above remarks were first written, in 1874, the author was severely criticized for what was called an "onslaught on co-operation." I, however, have been much misunderstood. I am a co-operator and believe in co-operation, though much more in industrial partnerships. All trade unionists are co-operators, as is shown by the fact that at nearly every Trade Union

Congress steps have been taken to further the co-operative movement, and at co-operative congresses trade union delegates are often officially present. In co-operation and industrial partnerships, as in trade unionism, lies the solution of many great social questions. The difference between the two kinds of association is that trade unionism tends to abolish middlemen by bringing capital and labour into close contact; co-operation by bringing them into coalescence. The former considers human nature as it is, and may therefore obtain its ends under existing social arrangements; co-operators argue as if human nature were as it ought to be, and the ultimate goal will not be in sight until the perfectibility of man is first reached. The co-operation, however, Mr. Thornton speaks of in his book "On Labour," is really socialism of the worse type. Now the British workman, though sympathizing with many socialistic views, is far from a socialist. He believes hard work should be recompensed with proportionately good pay, and is not prepared to accept a doctrine which says that, however much or however little he may work, his pay shall be the same, and that pay to consist, over and above his actual wants, of nothing but the gratitude of those around him. The trade unionist has no faith in a phantasy. He is not prepared to abandon his individuality or to shirk his responsibilities. He asks not for an equal division of wealth, but for its equitable division, in which the claims of capital, labour, and ability shall be duly acknowledged; and the results of his own thrift properly protected. The essence of trade unionism is sacrifice by the individual for the benefit of all: the essence of socialism is sacrifice by the industrious for the benefit of the indolent. The socialist would sacrifice others; the trade unionist sacrifices himself.

There is another economic effect of trade unionism which deserves at least a passing mention. The knowledge that men have the power to strike stimulates the inventive faculties of masters. A strike is not always confined in its effects to the particular branch of the trade that makes demands from the employer. A strike of puddlers enforces idleness on other ironworkers; while "finishers" cannot work if "fullers" won't. It is, therefore, to the advantage of the masters to have the various processes of manufacture as independent of each other as possible, so that if one department strikes, the necessity of another being idle may be reduced to a minimum. This is accomplished by the introduction of machinery, rendering less and less necessary the skill of workmen. Mr. Nasmyth, by mechanical contrivances, reduced the number of his men from 3000 to 1500 without reducing the production. It has been observed that, in consequence of almost all great strikes, the masters have set their wits to work, as the saying is, and have invented such improvements that they— and through them the world—have been very great gainers. A notable instance of this is found in the history of the struggle in 1851 of the engineers with their masters, to which reference has been already made. The process alluded to is going on at present very rapidly. In the iron industries especially, the improvements in material, and the almost daily introduction of newly invented labour-saving contrivances have resulted in one man being able to do what two and a half men were required to do thirty years ago, to say nothing of the important fact that the material is ten times more durable than it was, and the machines wear out much more slowly. These facts not only bear out the argument, but should induce the men to strengthen their unions, to compete with the displaced labour; and, wherever possible, reap two profits by becoming owners of the machines they construct, as was long ago suggested by the late Mr. John Kane.

Having shown, then, that trade unions cause material profit and an increase of general wealth, it remains, finally, to consider what are the effects of unions on those who belong to them; and if it can be shown that those effects are beneficial, then it will readily be acknowledged that they yield to society through their moral acts still more important services than they yield to commercial progress by their effects on trade.

It seems strange that in this enlightened age there are persons who believe that men can have more wages than are good for them. There is no such thing as being too well paid. The men who think so are, as a rule, those who are plentifully provided with the blessings of this life, and who opposed the movement in favour of universal education, because they objected to working men being too well educated, as it would make them discontented with their "station," as if there was such a thing as too much education. Orators who advocate these views quote startling facts by wholesale in support of their theory. We are told to notice the enormous increase in the consumption of whisky; but we are not reminded of the fact that in the middle class, where beer was formerly the principal beverage, the spirit bottle is now always at hand to welcome the friend or speed the parting guest. We hear a deal about the money squandered on the race-course; but why is it not impressed upon us that the increase in the number of depositors in the Post Office Savings Bank *alone* far surpasses the dreams of the most sanguine social reformers ? The men spend their time and their money in dog-fancying, says one; but he forgets that the magistrates of Cheshire are as famous for cock-fighting as the county is for cheese. A newspaper editor dwells with horror on the fact—or perhaps it is not a fact—that, somewhere or other, the miners go to work on horseback: it would have been more satisfactory if he had shown why the man at Birkenhead, who is said to be making between £400 and £500 a year by working at a Nasmyth's hammer, cannot ride with his grimy hands and face to business with the same propriety as the manager of a branch bank receiving only the same amount of salary. All such talk is no argument. There are foolish men and there are foolish masters. We have no wish to hold up the former as saints, and no desire to believe the latter are devils. All that is maintained here is that, though some evil may creep in with a rise of wages, as it seems to do with an increase of wealth, yet that good wages are a great blessing, and ought to be gladly welcomed by those who even have not yet reached that stage of morality of endeavouring to love their neighbours as themselves. At the very worst, all a man's increased wages are not squandered in wastefulness; and, after all, it is only what he ought to have saved that the imprudent man has spent in riotous living. Men who ought to know better do the same thing. The working man reads in his newspapers accounts of the disgraceful bankruptcies of noblemen and educated men of position, and he will not very much blame his fellow-workmen's indiscretion when he finds that those who should be patterns to the nation, with incomes in some cases of £80,000 a year, cannot keep the wolf from the door.

If the wages of working men rise so rapidly that the recipients do not know what to do with the surplus, there is this consolation, they will soon learn. Of all the agents of civilization money is the most powerful. When men see the comforts within their reach that hitherto they have only beheld afar off there can be no doubt they will buy them. Comforts once enjoyed are tardily relinquished. The man who has lived in a cottage has no desire to change it for a hovel, or he who has once been a prosperous workman will never long to join the militia or the army. With men in better homes there will be little crime; and without soldiers there can be no fighting. It is a well-established fact that in prosperous times recruits are difficult to find, and high wages, therefore, tend to bring about what Sir Charles Dilke wants when he says, "Rather than help the next generation to fight, I would prefer to so leave taxation as to make it hard for them to do so." It has been well said, "As the homes, so the people." There is no crime in happy homes, and if trade unionism can lift out from the depths of misery, and vice, and idleness those who are now a standing reproach to the civilized age in which we live, it will be entitled to an amount of gratitude from the country it has benefited, compared to which the praises sung in honour of the noblest achievements of the philanthropists, though uttered with the tongues of men and of angels, will be but as sounding brass and as tinkling cymbals.

The doctrine that that policy is best which gives the greatest 'good to the greatest number has become an axiom. Now, in every community the majority must always consist of working men and their families, and it does seem a natural way of proceeding that, if you give a greater happiness to a greater number, a step is being made towards realizing Bentham's celebrated dictum. The moral effects, then, of high wages are great. Of course they might be greater, but a little experience will bring that about. "Strikes, therefore, and the trade societies which render strikes possible, are for these various reasons not a mischievous, but, on the contrary, a valuable part of the existing machinery of society."

It would be a work of supererogation to discuss here the great advantages of more leisure to the working class, but as it is one of the objects of a trade union to obtain shorter hours, and as the realization of such a policy has a very beneficial effect on those who belong to trade societies, the question cannot be passed over without a few words.* The advantages of recreation are acknowledged, but few steps are taken to afford the means to indulge in it. It is still quite common for young girls to walk early in the mornings—winter and summer—a distance of three or four miles, carrying their whole day's provender with them, work, standing in a factory, all day long, and then walk home at night.

---

* It has already been pointed out (see page 89) that a long hour's day means dear labour. Mr. Thorold Rogers has shown in his recent work that it is also incompatible with good workmanship. Speaking of the excellent masonry of Merton Tower, Oxford, four hundred years old, he says, "I am persuaded that such perfect masonry would have been incompatible with a long hour's day!"

It is too much to expect these, immediately they get
home, to rush off to the "Institute"—perhaps a mile
or two away—to be taught the mysteries of knitting or
the history of Joseph and his brethren. Their whole
time is spent in working or sleeping, with perhaps a
little flirting on Sunday with lads similarly placed to
themselves; and any action of the unions that can lop
off another hour a day which these poor creatures may
devote to improving or enjoying themselves will be
very beneficial indeed.*

The men, too, in various trades are not only showing
a desire to generally improve themselves, but to obtain
a deeper knowledge of their own particular trades.
This was mentioned in the first chapter, but it will
bear repeating here. Some time ago, Mr. Wilcock,
the then president of the London Royal Lodge of the
General Union of Carpenters, initiated a series of
lectures to its members, and the president himself
delivered one on "The Knowledge and Use of Scales as
Applied to the Building Trade." The following month
Mr. Disc gave a lecture on freehand drawing. At present, in London, there are several technical classes
conducted by artisans, and the City of Guilds Institute,
as well as the Polytechnic Institution, and the Artisans'
Technical Association, are doing much to promote that
object. There can be no doubt as to the effect of thus
teaching men that what their hands find to do should
be done with all their might, however weak that might
may be. Men are made for something better than to
be hewers of wood and drawers of water; and Jeanie
Dean's father was not far wrong when he said: "If ye

* In many trades children thirteen years of age still work ten
hours a day.

neglect your warldly duties . . . what confidence have
I that ye mind the greater matters that concern salva-
tion ? God knows our bowies, and our pipkins, and
our draps o' milk, and our bits o' bread, are nearer and
dearer to us than the bread of life." Indeed, the plan
of lecturing just referred to rapidly bears fruit, and
some of the members of the union mentioned have, on
account of their superior knowledge of their trade, been
appointed clerks of the works and head foremen to
some of the principal firms in England. Other unions
have similar means of improving their members and
raising their tastes ; and it is to be hoped that ere long
the practice will be universal. The more time the unions
can obtain for their men to do this (and workmen thus
educated will be better workmen) the better it will be ;
and it is, therefore, for the unions to struggle with all
the means in their power in order that the men may get
as much wages as they can (without infringing upon
that limit when their productions would be unremunerative) for as little work as possible, performed with
a minimum of inconvenience.

Indeed, the great advantage of union men over non-
union men is being discovered by the masters, and the
masters are beginning to acknowledge the fact. A
Liverpool carpenter recently told the author that the
masters knew the union men were the best workmen,
and that it was a regular thing to give them one penny
per hour more than the rate fixed upon by the society.*
This is not surprising, as no man can be an amalgamated carpenter unless he "be in good health, have
worked five years at the trade, be a good workman, of
steady habits and good moral character." If, too, a

* The master tailors have publicly borne similar testimony.

man has been dismissed through misconduct,* such as
drunkenness or disorderly conduct, he is not entitled to
donation until he has again been in employment two
months at the average rate of wages paid by the town
in which he is working; while if he even boasts of his
independence towards his employer or employers, on
account of his being a member of the society, "he is
fined half a crown." Other unions have similar safeguards. Unionists are not desirous of having incompetent or unsteady workmen as associates. They can
see that such men do as much to lower wages as anything else. The good workmen know this, and they
crowd into the unions as fast as they can. Of course it
is not maintained here that all unionist workmen are
proficient. There are, as a matter of fact, several
unionists who are not good workmen; but there are
few good workmen who are not unionists. The men
out of union are, for "the most part, either inferior
workmen, employed on inferior work at reduced rates,
or those who have belonged to it and are erased. Of
these last, some left because they did not wish to pay
to it, or, indeed, to anything else that they could avoid;
and the rest, by far the greatest number, are those who
have been erased for non-payment through their unfortunate habits of intemperance, which left them no
means of paying." The trade unions may fairly consider whether or not it comes within their province to
take even stronger measures to ensure the efficiency of
their members. A "more definite standard of efficiency"
than at present might be decided upon, so that a man's

* Workmen are also dismissed from their unions for incompetency, and may be even prosecuted for violence by their own
society.

union ticket would be a standard of competency, and accepted as such by the employers. An idea similar to this seems to have occurred to the Glasgow engine-keepers, as, at a meeting September 26th, 1874, it was resolved to petition Parliament to appoint a board of examiners for the purpose of granting certificates of competency to engine-keepers in Great Britain and Ireland; and, failing in this, it was decided that a local board of examiners should be appointed. Almost every year the Trade Unions Congress formally urges a similar view, and it is to the credit of Mr. John Burnett and Mr. Thos. Burt that they so persistently insist that Parliament should take the matter in hand. If something of this kind were practicable in every trade — and the unions have an excellent organization for carrying out the suggestion—it would be of infinite benefit to the community. The masters would readily acknowledge certificates of proficiency issued by the unions, because they accept the principle now, by giving higher wages and more responsible positions to those unionists who have held office in their societies, naturally concluding that when a workman has earned the respect of his peers, he is also entitled to the confidence of his superiors; and, what seems very strange, in cases of disputes between masters and non-unionist workmen, the latter very often select a unionist as their representative at the board of arbitration. It may be added that the unions are showing a laudable desire to take a high tone in regard to this matter. They have over and over again protested against the "scamping" of work and cheating of purchasers, against jerry building, sizing cotton, etc., etc. They are not "the fault of the artisan—they are his misfortune," says an official report,

M

and continues : "We know from experience that the properly trained and highly skilled workman is the first to suffer by the shameful process. When circumstances press him into this circle of competition he has to undergo a second apprenticeship to acquire this sleight-of-hand system, during which he earns less wages." Mr. Thomas Hughes thinks the unions "are powerful enough now to insist, if they choose to do so, that no unionist shall work where such practices prevail." Mr. Thorold Rogers takes a similar view, adding that the men should protect the public, denouncing and exposing "dishonest and scantling work." I may add that the desire of the workmen in the direction above indicated is shown by the objection on the part of artisans to clerks and others studying in technical classes, lest such should learn just sufficient to be dabbler at the trade, and thus cause to be thrown in the market a quantity of incompetent labour. The same feeling is shown in the desire for sound regulations in regard to apprentices, for it is obvious that any skilled trade not protected by an apprenticeship system must always occupy a low status.

The most important educational work which the trade unions are performing is that of familiarizing the workmen—and, for that matter, the master as well—with the true relations of capital to labour. The men must learn to submit to reductions when it is proper they should do so ; and the masters must learn to abandon that dominant spirit they assume whenever an advance is respectfully solicited. An ironmaster in the north of England writes to the author : "I have had twenty years of pretty close acquaintanceship with both artisans and labourers of all kinds, and I know many of them have much sounder views of common-sense political economy than the middle classes in general hold. I look upon trade unions as admirable training schools for the workmen, where they will soon outgrow their heresies on the subject of capital and labour; whereas, if they are browbeaten and scolded in a violent manner, they will begin—as some of them, I fear, have already —to think that masters are to be regarded as their natural enemies, and treated accordingly. The uneducated workmen are, as a rule, a rather violent set of fellows, it must be admitted; but I can see that, under the training and leadership of the foremost men in the unions, these are fast becoming a very small minority, as they are very plainly and forcibly told that the old way of settling disputes with their employers is about the very worst that could be adopted. This, coming from men of their own class, they are daily becoming more and more ready to listen to with respect, which would not be the case if it emanated from the employers' class, whom they have good grounds for regarding with distrust and suspicion. I know enough of the unprincipled conduct of the employers, through their agents in our iron industry, to understand and excuse much in the conduct of the unionists that would be indefensible on any other grounds than those of extreme injustice and most heartless provocation—not that the employers have directly perpetrated such things personally, but they must be held responsible, seeing that they have seldom or ever taken the trouble to find out the rights and wrongs of disputed points; but in ninety-nine out of one hundred cases the underlings have been left to take their own course and represent their own case as, of course, decidedly angelic. The unions have done

immense service in bringing about a different state of
things, and, to my certain knowledge, it has been due
to the influence of the leaders of the unions that the
system of arbitration has been adopted lately in so
many industries; and this, bear in mind, in spite of
the dogged resistance of many of the employers, who
don't like the system, as I have heard them say,
because it puts a weapon into the men's hands to fight
them with when a dispute arises about the rate of
wages."

This passage is given, not only because it contains
some cogent reasons in favour of the present argument,
but because, coming from where it does, it justifies
what might otherwise appear as the too strong language
used against the employers in the course of this essay.
Of course such strictures do not apply to all capitalists,
and they are only directed against those whom they
concern. It is well known that there are others who
—but good wine needs no bush. Combination in bad
hands may mean something very terrible—such as a
strike—but in good hands it may mean calm delibera-
tion and prudent counsel. When Mr. Macdonald
induced some men to accept a reduction of 20 per
cent., he was doing more than giving them friendly
advice. He naturally gave them reasons for pursuing
such a policy, and such reasons were not only a
lesson in prudence and forbearance, but the solution
of a problem in political economy. The very terms
upon which an arbitration shall be conducted are
pregnant with useful instruction such as the men have
never received before.

Not only is the influence of trade unions of such
a nature as to make men better economists, but it

also has a tendency to make them better politicians, using the word in its proper and not in a party sense. A great deal of the time of the legislature is, and has been, and will again be, taken up in discussing measures specially affecting the labouring population; the unions debating upon abstruse questions, and deciding upon vigorous and intelligent parliamentary action. They think—and rightly so—that this can best be done by having men of their own order, and practically acquainted with their wants and wishes, elected as their representatives in the House of Commons. The unions have done good work in parliamentary action in the past. Indeed, when it is remembered that all the disputes, desires, and wishes of the men have always been inquired into, decided upon, and legislated for by the masters, the wonder is, not that the men have obtained so little, but that they have achieved so much. The opposition to measures which the men had initiated, or for which they clamoured, has been something stupendous, and they may, therefore, with pride contemplate their victories. It was the unions who cried aloud for the Factory Acts; it was, and is now, the unions who demand laws to enforce the better ventilation of mines, and to secure miners against accidents, caused by a selfish economy. It was the unions, and not the masters, who asked for the inquiry in 1850; and when the Act which was passed in consequence of that inquiry proved insufficient, it was again the unions who, in 1852, demanded further inquiry, the result of which was the more complete measure of 1855. Who was it demanded compulsory education, and demanded it in opposition to the masters? It was the workmen in combination,

who, suffering from the accidents of ignorance, were
well alive to the blessings of intelligence and education.   So keenly did they feel on this point, that
in a petition to Parliament, signed by 50,000 persons,
they expressed their willingness to pay for that which
they prayed by contributions from their wages, on
the very natural condition that some of their order
should sit on the governing body.   Not only have
they fought and won in the House of Commons, but
they have often been placed on the defensive in the
Law Courts, and, with a few exceptions, have won
there also.   When the masters, with a tenacity the
wickedness of which is only equalled by its audacity,
took from the men, under the name of forfeits, one-
fifth of the payment on the coal raised — that is,
one-fifth of their wages—Parliament stepped in and
ordered the appointment of a " check weigher," to
be chosen by the men.   So grasping, however, were
the employers—so determined to rob the collier of
one-fifth of his wages—that they evaded the law by
forbidding the man chosen of the men to enter their
premises.   Mr. Normansell, who had been chosen by
the men, was ejected eighteen times, and carried his
case from court to court, finally winning the day in the
Court of Queen's Bench.   The old spirit again showed
its head in an attempt to send Mr. Halliday to a felon's
cell ; and although there are masters and men hoping
and sighing for the good time coming, yet there is
sadly too much evidence that intolerance is not dead,
but sleepeth.

Although the unions have done such glorious work
in the past, there is ample left yet to be accomplished.
The masters, true to instinct and tradition, displayed a

warlike front in the memorial which the National
Federation of Associated Employers of Labour presented
to the Home Secretary. "Men have been convicted,"
says Mr. Henry Crompton, "for simply standing still
in the street, when there was no attempt at intimidation
or coercion, without word or gesture having been used.
Seven men were sent to jail in one batch in Perth for
doing nothing more than this picketing—that is, the
men waiting for a fellow-workman, accosting him, and
endeavouring to influence him by argument or per-
suasion, has been declared to be a crime by a competent legal tribunal. On one occasion seven women
were sent to prison for shouting at a man who was
walking away from the pit where he had been working,
and who is reported to have said, in his evidence, 'I
heard shouting, but I cannot say where it came from.'"
Men have been imprisoned for breaking a contract to save
their lives. "It takes days," says Sir Wm. Harcourt,
"and sometimes weeks, to examine a ship, and we have
a law which keeps a seaman in prison under a labour
contract until an investigation has proved her to be unseaworthy. In one case the men were kept in prison
during the process of the investigation, and when found
innocent were discharged without any compensation for
the false imprisonment they had undergone." A man
who broke a bad bargain was liable to imprisonment; the
master who did so was merely subjected to a pecuniary
consideration. In the face of these disgraceful proceedings, were not the men justified in demanding an
amendment of the Master and Servant Act, and in
asking for a repeal of the "Criminal Law Amendment
Act"? and the law was amended in these respects by
the direct action of the trade unions. The federated

employers announced their intention to oppose the efforts of the men in their attempts to obtain both.

Again, there are the laws on conspiracy. Attention has already been called to the vague and unintelligible nature of these laws. They are a puzzle to the shrewdest lawyers, and hardly any two judges on the Bench are agreed as to what criminal conspiracy really is. Attempts have been made to bring the officers of unions within the statute, and although no jury has yet been found to convict them, yet on the slighest provocation the masters have hoped, by continued prosecutions—paid for out of the imperial exchequer—so to hamper and harass the unions, who are mulcted in large sums of money for the defence of their officers, that in time they would become tired of the game. The men think this state of things should be altered; and here again they know well enough that a strong opposition would be made. So, too, the Truck Act, which fined a master £20 for the infringement of an Act—by which infringement the master made £30,000 a year out of his men, and could, therefore, well afford to pay the penalty—was to be denounced by the men as unjust and iniquitous, and upheld by the masters—naturally—as the pink of perfection. The Factory Bills and others, too, were an eyesore to the federated masters, and, indeed, everything that was for the amelioration of the working classes was to be opposed to the bitter end by the union of those who denounce unionists; and this body, by an "intrigue," as Mr. Frederic Harrison calls it, succeeded in postponing legislation by the appointment of a needless Parliamentary Commission.

All these reforms that the trade unionists demand

are such as will remove from the statute book all that
savours of class legislation. No new privilege—except
that of freedom, which has hitherto been withheld—
is asked to be invented on the workman's behalf. The
labourer does not need, and therefore does not desire,
special legislation. All he asks is, that the remaining
shreds of inequality in the treatment of employers and
employed shall be removed, and that before the law he
may stand face to face with his master on equal terms.
There are, as Mr. Henry Crompton has pointed out, in
the statute book a vast number of the most extraordinary laws intended to crush all combined action
and freedom of expression. They have not been put
in force for many years, but other obsolete acts have,
and those may at any moment. If that were done, they
would probably render all trade societies and most
political associations criminal. The British workman
demands that these should be repealed. He asks no
favour. Knowing justice to be on his side, he demands that it shall not be withheld. The thinking
working man, for instance, cannot understand why
there should be such a law of conspiracy as at present
exists. If an act be not a crime when committed by
one person, it can hardly be a crime when thought
of by two, or two hundred; while, if it be a crime
when committed by one, surely it is *à fortiori* a crime
when committed by more than one, conspiracy or
no conspiracy. If a man, or men, of whatever class,
be guilty of a crime, surely there is at present—or if
not, there soon can be—sufficient law to punish him
without disgracing our Statute Book with obnoxious,
partial, and invidious Acts. It is an opinion of some
eminent jurists that conspiracy ought only to be a

crime in the case of treason. The Conspiracy Laws at
present, too, are dangerously vague, and the various
constructions that can be put upon them are often con-
tradictory. Truly it is difficult to conceive that there
should be any special laws relating to the employed
and their employers. The law of contract ought to be
. enough for all purposes. Laws relating to violence
and intimidation, to be just, must apply to the whole
community, and must not be directed against trade
unionists alone; while the law which singles out the
workman *alone* for imprisonment for breach of contract
can have but one effect: "It gives no protection to
good masters, but means of oppression to bad ones."
In fighting for these reforms, trade unionists are not
only striving for what will benefit themselves, but, by
diffusing a spirit of liberalism and justice, are bestowing
an incalculable benefit upon their fellow-men.

The unions are doing good work in another direction.
Their attention is not solely confined to questions
affecting capital and labour. The trade unions not
only wish the labourers to be good workmen—they are
also determined to make them good citizens. They
are anxious to do away with all class distinctions. It
is not forgotten that at the first attempt at arbitration when the miners in South Staffordshire met the
masters, the latter were seated comfortably at a table,
with pens, ink, note paper, etc., and a chairman duly
installed; but the men were directed to a bench at the
bottom of the room, as though they were culprits
awaiting trial, rather then fellow-men assembled to
agree upon a contract to the benefit of all concerned.
All such snobbery is to be annihilated. The men are
beginning to feel "the glorious privilege of being

independent." It is time they did. Nothing tends so much to degrade a class as the knowledge that it is dependent.* The day has gone by when a man must feel loyal and dutiful to another simply because he has been born on his estate, or because he works in his factory. The men are willing enough to receive the ambassador of the employer with all due respect, but they demand (on the peril of a strike) that their own delegates shall be equally well received. It is now acknowledged that the demeanour most fitting towards the poor is that which is most fitting towards every one. The leaders of the unions have perceived that the general tendency of human progress is in this direction, and they have determined not to oppose, but to assist it. Their demands, therefore, are for the assimilation of the county to the borough franchise; a redistribution of seats; payment of election expenses out of the rates, so that if being a labourer be no reason why a man should be sent to Parliament, it equally shall be no reason why he should not; a general appointment of stipendiary magistrates, so that justice may be more fairly meted than at Chipping Norton and elsewhere. Steps to bring about such reforms as these are vigorously taken, to say nothing about protests against governmental extravagance, unseaworthy ships, tax on

---

* Last year the millers of London began an agitation for a Saturday half-holiday. Those, however, who took part in the proceedings were obliged to keep their names secret for fear of dismissal by their employers, and it was explained that "not being members of any society they would in such a case have nothing to fall back upon." Their best policy is to join the Millers' Union, and thereby secure themselves something to fall back upon, and so become independent and self-reliant.

railway passengers, and clamours for direct taxation,
working-men's trains, disestablishment and disendow-
ment of the Church, the appropriation of endowments,
and other things too numerous to mention. The trade
unions have done great service in pursuing this policy.
Indeed, it is not too much to say that, had the agricultural labourers been in union a quarter of a century
ago, there would long ere this have been a complete
reform in the land laws, the commons would have been
preserved, waste lands have been cultivated, the generation now dying out would have been educated, and the
material and moral progress of the country would have
been much greater than one at first seems inclined to
acknowledge. As Mr. Frederic Harrison points out,
another sphere of action awaits trade unionists. "It is
the great field of local self-government. There is the
true sphere of the working man's activity. The health-
fulness and good management of their cities, towns,
and villages should demand their attention. It is the
condition of their large cities which affects the great
masses of population rather than it does the rich, who
can afford to withdraw themselves from their midst. . . .
They must be town councillors, members of school
boards, and even mayors of boroughs in which they,
reside."

It is not only part of the policy of trade unions to
demand as rights those privileges which are now withheld from them, but also to render their members fit
to exercise those rights. It has already been shown that
civility to their employers, as well as sobriety, are
essential before a man can become a practical trade
unionist; while "any member causing a quarrel, swearing, or using abusive language in any of the society's

meetings," is fined. Rules of order are strictly enforced, and if members are disorderly they are expelled the room. Any conduct of a "very aggravated nature" is specially dealt with. Care is taken that the benefits of the society shall have no appearance of charitable relief —as, indeed, they are not—and "any member upbraid- ing another for receiving any benefits of the society" is liable to a somewhat heavy fine—as heavy a fine, indeed, as is imposed when one member strikes another. Means are also taken to ensure the honesty of the members. Any member convicted by a court of justice is liable to exclusion from the society, or such other punishment as the branch to which he belongs may deem fit. Glancing over a list of expulsions from the Engineers' Society, are found the following reasons for expelling members :

"For imposing on the society while receiving sick pay."
"For imposing on the society while working."
"For incompetency."
"For misappropriation of the society's funds."
"For not refunding a donation improperly received."
"For drawing donation when working."
"For perjury."
"For attempting to defraud a member."
"For dishonesty."

With such a power as this it is evident the incompetent, the dishonest, the drunken, and the idle must be driven from the sunshine of unionism into the bitter cold regions of non-unionism. When men see rules and subscribe to them against certain practices, they (for use doth breed a habit in a man) look upon those prac- tices as *wrong*, and they soon become in every way better men. Not only do the unions take steps to prevent evil, they exert themselves to promote good.

Perhaps enough has already been said on this head, and therefore here it may be sufficient to give as a sample a sentence from one of the manifestoes of the Amalgamated Society of Carpenters: "We shall be faithless to our fellow-workmen if we omit to record our honest conviction that this much-to-be-desired condition must be preceded by the equally universal spread of the principles of economy and sobriety, which would be accelerated by our meeting for business in public halls or private rooms, where, by the establishment of libraries, and listening to the voice of the lecturer on all subjects connected with our interests, we and our sons should become respectful and respected, and make rapid progress in the onward march of reform."

A great deal is made by anti-unionists of the notion that when a man joins a union he loses his liberty and becomes a slave to the union agent or the union executory. It may be very properly replied that a man, if he likes, has a right to give up his liberty. Even Mr. Gladstone acknowledged this in a speech already referred to. The argument, however, if such it can be called, is wrong in fact. The workman in delegating the task of asking for more wages, instead of asking for them personally, is no more giving up his liberty than a client is in hiring an advocate to plead for him to a jury. The men in a union come together of their own accord; they do not so, and do not remain so, unless they think it to their advantage; and they can leave the society whenever they like. To say that this is giving up one's liberty is the same in principle as saying that a man in obeying certain laws of his country, of which he disapproves, is giving up his liberty. It may as well be argued, for instance, that the members of the Peace Society in paying their shares towards the expenses of the Egyptian war, of which the said members disapproved, are giving up their liberty to refuse these payments. It has always been an acknowledged principle that a man may voluntarily submit to certain restrictions on his liberty for the common good. Thus a man must drive on the left-hand side of the road, and he must not erect noxious works in crowded neighbourhoods. Children must be educated, and too many persons must not crowd into one sleeping-room. The trade unionist, too, is much freer in regard to his union than is the citizen in regard to the State. It is with great difficulty the latter can throw off his obligations, and then but to rest under fresh restrictions; but the former can do so with the greatest facility, though, for reasons mentioned in a former chapter, he seldom avails himself of the opportunity.

In addition to the huge moral effects which have been already noticed, there are a crowd of smaller ones, that in the aggregate are very formidable. The assistance afforded to emigrants has been already touched upon. It is worthy of note that during times of distress union men seldom apply for parochial relief, and according to a competent authority trade unions have kept hundreds of thousands of persons off the poor rates. Of course this influence is chiefly due to that portion of the trade union which is more properly a friendly society. Too much stress must not be laid upon the half-suggestion contained in the last chapter, that perhaps it would be better if the societies contented themselves with the business of trade unions, leaving the work of friendly societies to be accomplished by another organization.

Inasmuch, however, as most trade unions are benefit
societies, they have all the influence (and none of the
flummery) which flows from those bodies. To teach
men to prepare for a rainy day, to lay by for old age, to
protect themselves from poverty in case of accident or
failing health, loss of tools, etc., and to reward merit
and inculcate the principle of brotherly love and
benevolence, are surely laudable objects, and so long as
the criteria are sound, they cannot help but have a
good influence upon those who are prudent enough to
deny themselves to-day, in order that they may enjoy
to-morrow.

These societies, too, are exceedingly useful in the
mass of valuable statistics they collect. The death
rates and the causes of death in various trades point to
a field in which medical men may work to great
advantage; while the fluctuations in the rates of wages,
and the gradual shortening of hours present an equally
interesting problem to political economists. This information, too, is given for, comparatively speaking,
small districts, and the problems referred to can therefore be studied when local influences interfere with
general laws. Altogether there is ample food for both
the student, the philosopher, and the statesman, in the
vast amount of literature that is annually issued by the
trade societies of Great Britain; and which, by the
way, must keep employed a great number of printers,
thus benefiting a trade by the mere action of recording
the experience of their existence.

Not long ago a committee of the British Association
for the Advancement of Science was appointed to
consider the great question that has been discussed by
such incompetent hands in these pages. This com-

mittee, having studied the "extensive literature which has accumulated on the subject," and having had a conference between masters and men, was unable to arrive at any better conclusion than that the "questions are as yet but insufficiently appreciated, especially by the parties most interested," and could suggest no plan by which the question might be settled. They therefore recommended "the reappointment of the committee, with instructions to renew the conference already inaugurated, and to report on the general question." When failure characterizes efforts in such a quarter, what can be expected from the attempts of the author of this paper? He, however, will yield to none in admiration of trade unions and faith in their mission. However inadequately the idea may be expressed in this work, it seems to the writer that opposing trade unionism is fighting against the inevitable. It has been pointed out that combination amongst workmen has existed ever since men had the intelligence to understand that they were oppressed by those whose position gave them the power to oppress. The power to combine became more and more generally acknowledged, until at length, in spite of unjust and partial laws, trade unions became a fact. From combinations against oppression they developed into associations having for their object the amelioration of the condition of the working class. It has also been shown that the organization of a trade union is pre-eminently fitted to carry out that object, and as proof of that it has been argued: 1st, That trade unions have succeeded in raising wages and reducing the number of working hours. 2nd, That these reforms do not benefit the labourer at the cost of either the capitalist or the consumer; as,

N

between certain limits, it is found that high pay and the prospect of an early cessation from work are such incentives to industry that the produce of labour is actually greater than under a system of long hours and low pay. 3rd, That the workmen have such confidence in the benefits they derive from union, that, after the experience of " half a millennium," they are crowding into societies, into unions, in a greater ratio every year. 4th, That their declared object is to prevent strikes, and substitute arbitrations; and although the latter mode of settling disputes is often proposed by the men and refused by the masters, it is seldom proposed by the masters and still less often refused by the men. It has been argued further, that such being the objects of trade unions, and such their success in obtaining those objects, the influence of that success must be very beneficial; 1st, Because high wages means increased comforts, which are not only a social but a commercial advantage. High wages means increased production, also the double blessing just mentioned. 2nd, Because high wages does not mean enhanced prices, but the contrary. 3rd, Because the principles of trade unionism teach men the prudence of denying themselves something to-day in order that they may have greater advantages to-morrow; and the duty of self-sacrifice, by calling upon them to contribute, out of their meagre wealth, towards the alleviation of the sufferings of their fellow-men. 4th, Because trade unions endeavour to obtain for the working classes more leisure for recreation and study. 5th, Because, by lectures and other means, the unions endeavour to make their members better workmen; and by rules which stigmatize and punish the idle, the vicious, and the incompetent, do all in their power to make workmen better citizens. 6th, Unionism makes men better politicians; while it teaches them to submit to unchangeable laws, it shows them how to take advantage of these laws. It thus makes them independent, and enables them to demand as their right what has hitherto been withheld from them. It makes clear to them that capital does not make the man, and that a labourer is no worse because he works. Jack is as good as his master; and the men know that if employers would only acknowledge this—if they would only meet their workmen as men on an equal footing with themselves, and discuss the wages system with them, as the late Mr. Brassey, Mr. E. Akroyd, Mr. W. E. Forster, and others were in the habit of doing—then strikes would be impossible.

It is really difficult to conceive how an institution with such noble objects, having attained those objects, can be anything but a great blessing to the community in which it is placed. There are some persons, however, who can find a dark side to everything, and because trade unions have sent three of their own class to Parliament, these persons imagine that the destruction of the world is not far off. What will such people think when trade unionism extends its influence to domestic servants; and the freakish clause in the Employers and and Workman Act which excludes them from the benefits of its provision is repealed? To those, on the other hand, who look at the bright side of things, there appears in the future everything that can be hoped and wished, nothing that needs be feared. Good will always prevail over evil in the end, and whatever evil there may be in trade unionism will soon die for want of sustenance.

In contemplating the great future which is in store
for trade unionism, the present unhappy relations that
exist between employers and employed must not be
forgotten. One of the steps to be taken first, because
of its importance, is that which brings together the
two classes of society in harmony and good will. As
Mr. Henry Broadhurst told the Paris Conference of
workmen last year (1883), working men should raise
themselves, not by depressing others, but acting with
them in friendliness. The present state is one of
all-abhorred war, with lucid intervals of peace. This
is slowly—too slowly—passing away ; and every means
should be taken to bring about a happier and a brighter
time. The evils are old, and the experience is great.
What is wanted is the intelligence to discern the
evils, the charity to acknowledge them, and the wisdom
to remedy them. "Light, more light" should be the
desire of all. There are already signs of day. The
dawn is visible. Some of the most intelligent of the
masters have already acknowledged the justice of
unionism, and others are day by day following that
example. Support comes whence least expected. The
candidate for the throne of France, who of all others
in a similar position is best fitted to be a king, has
written to his countrymen a fair and honest description of trade unions in England. He has done so in
the hope that the working men of his own country
will adopt the same means of improving their condition, and of becoming more and more useful to
themselves and the world. It is hoped that there is no
presumption in saying that others, like Mr. Thornton,
have viewed the promised land. Afar off it may truly
be, but still promised. In that happy region the

labourer is worthy of his hire. There are no animosities, no struggles between class and class; no wars or rumours of war. The men have long ago discovered what is a fair day's work, and the masters have found a means of ascertaining what is a fair day's wages. There, men—even working men—are known as men, having a "God-created form," and there each has his own reward.

> "Wishes o'erjoyed with humble things,
> A rank adjudged by toil-worn merit;
>   Content that from employment springs,
>   A heart that in his labour sings;
> A heritage it seems to me,
> A king might wish to hold in fee." *

Trade unionism, then, has a great future before it. Its ultimate result cannot be otherwise than to convince both employer and employed that they are the truest friends, each of the other, for each derives his revenue from the other. The prosperity of the country is greatly due to the influence of unions on trade, and therefore that influence benefits the capitalist as well as the workman. Indeed, it cannot be too often remembered that in the exchange that takes place between master and man, the one ought not to be expected to reluctantly yield what the other imperiously demands; but that each should give what he can best spare for that which he most wants. The master parts with his capital because he wants the man's labour, and the man parts with his labour because he wants a part of the master's capital. There is a mutual obligation, a fact which has hitherto been too often forgotten. The

* J. Russell Lowell.

men, however, have not forgotten it; nor was it likely
they would. Could it be thought for one moment that
the men who have made England what she is, who have
honeycombed this country with great cities, who have
cultivated every inch of its cultivated area—could it be
thought for one moment that, knowing how much they
had done towards this, and how few of the benefits of
it all were awarded them, they would lie down, submit,
and remain silent and patient for ever under such per-
petual exclusion from participation in the fruits of
their labour? What did the workmen do to remove
that deep and widespread feeling of injustice? The
past history of their country told them of secret conspiracies, of midnight drillings, of rick burnings, and
of riots. These things, however, seemed to them the
barbarous customs of a barbarous age; and they found
in their unions that strength which singleness of purpose and a thorough faith in the justice of a cause alone
can give. They believed that the principles of trade
unionism were sound. They believe now that they are
as sound as those of any other institution, and the
unionists are to be congratulated on having for years
kept the light burning in the midst of the dismal dark-
ness that surrounded them. They are to be honoured
very much for having, through a great deal of evil
report and very little of good report, through much
tribulation, and when in a small minority, kept up the
advocacy of principles which they believed to be true,
and which the people of this country will more and
more come to believe to be true.

INDEX.

A

Agricultural labourers, 21, 47, 53, 81, 107
Aldershot shoemakers, 85
Allan, William, 92, 103
Alliance cabinet-makers, 65
Amalgamated Boot and Shoe-makers, 54
Amalgamated Carpenters and Joiners, 45
Amalgamated Engineers, origin of, 32 (and note); description of, 48
Amalgamated Tailors, 68
Amalgamation, beginning of, 48, 53
Applegarth, Robert, 101, 103
Apprentices, 114
Arbitrations, 96; first proposed by the unions, 101
Arch, Joseph, 92
Aristotle on the common-wealth, 2
Association, first signs of, 8

B

Bad rules in unions, 114, 118, 121
Bailey, E. W., 61
Bakers (Scotch), 33

Bassett, John, on foreign manufactures, 19
"Benefits," 111
Bill of Mr. Neale, M.P., 36
Bill to protect trade union funds, 37
Birkenhead Trade Council, 45
Birtwistle, Thomas, 93
Black Death, the, 5, 8
Boilermakers, the, 35
Brassey, Sir Thomas, 69, 137
Brentano, Dr. Lujo, 11
Bricklayers, the, 74, 118, 121
Bright, John, 83, 91, 100
British Association, the, 176
Broadhead, 91 (note)
Broadhurst, Henry, 61, 92, 180
Burnett, John, 61, 92, 93, 161
Burt, Thomas, 92, 93, 94, 161

C

Cabinet-makers, in Antwerp, etc., 65
Cabmen, the Paris, 60
Canada Works, Birkenhead, wages at, 69
Cairns, Professor, 140
Capitalist artisan, the, 4
Certificates of competency, 161
Chamberlain, Joseph, 147

Child labour, long hours of, 17, 185

Coal price of, 141, 171; and wages, 145, 146

Coalowners, 100

Church, the, and serfdom, 3

Coinage, debasement of, 14

Colliers, West Yorkshire, 145

Combinations, first signs of, 8; forbidden, 11; of saddlers suppressed, 11; severe laws against, 15; legislation against, 18; laws against repealed, 19; become a necessity, 24; become legal, 35; first begun by employers, 31; of employers, 97

Compositors, London, 45; 51 (note)

Confiscation of the guilds, 14

Conference, the first, 35; its Bill, 37; of unionists at Paris, 61

Conspiracy, laws on, 168

Co-operation, 103, 148

Corn laws, repeal of the, 22

Craft guilds, 9

Crompton, Henry, 167, 169

Creasy, Sir E. S., 3

Criminal Law Amendment Act, 167

D

Daily News, anecdote from, 99

Debasement of the coinage, 14

Dennys, Mr., 87

Dilke, Sir Charles, 156

Dissolution of the monasteries, 14

Domestic servants, 179

Domestic system, decline of, 24

Donation, origin of, 30

Dunning, J. T., 43, 99, 112, 120

E

Eight hours, a day's work, 14

Emancipation of serfs, 3, 11

Employers, attempts to reduce wages, 145; combinations of, 97; and employed, decisions on acts relating to, 39; law amended, 39; federation of, 108; have seldom raised wages unasked, 77; strike against each other, 100

Engineers, 161; society of, indictment against, 32; reasons for expulsion from society of, 173

Errors of unionists, 91

Expulsion from a union, reasons for, 173

F

Factory Acts, dawn of, 17

Factory system, rise of, 25

Fawcett, Henry, 43, 47, 146, 148

Federal principle, 53

Federation of employers, 108, 167

Federation of trades, 59

Financial Reform Association, 127, 129

Foreign competition, 138

Foreign manufactures, outcry against, 19

France, trade unions in, 62

Freemasons, the, 9

G

"Geo-chenk," 30

Giffen, Robert, 70

Girdleston, Canon, 98

Gladstone, W. E., 118 (note), 119, 120, 174

Glassmakers, the, 105
" Good old times," the, 2
Gostrick, Joseph, 44
Green, J. R., 16
Grostête, a serf, 12
Guilds, 9, 25; confiscation of, 14
Gurney's, Russell, Act, 42

H

Halliday, Mr., 93, 166
Hand Mule Spinners' Association, 54
Harcourt, Sir William, 143 (note), 167
Harrison, Frederic, 41, 44, 55, 104, 136, 145, 168, 172
Heatherly, Mrs., 62
Henry II., alluded to, 2, 5
High wages, benefits of, 130; not unremunerative, 135; do not cause increased prices, 141; effects of, 155
Hornby v. Close, 35; petition to parliament, 38
Hours of labour, 85; shorter hours, more work, 89; benefits of short, 157
House painters, alliance of, 68
Howell, George, 55, 66 (note), 104
Hughes, Thomas, 162

I

Income of the people, 72
Indictment against engineers, 42
Industry, legal restrictions on, 21
International Society, the, 59
Invention stimulated by strikes, 153

Ironfounders' Society, the, 26, 55
Ironmaster, an, on trade unionism, 162
Iron shipbuilders, 35

J

Justices, power to fix wages, 18

K

Kane, John, 92, 93
Kettle, Rupert, 95, 101
King, J. R., 116

L

Laws, unequal, 35
Labourers not subjects, but "fragments," 2
Labour, future price of never fixed, 102
Lectures to artisans, 158
Limitation of work, 113
Lock-out, the agricultural, 78
Lollards, the, 12
Luddite rising, the, 24 (note)

M

Macclesfield weavers, 78
Machinery, introduction of, 23
Macaulay, Lord, 3, 19
Macdonald, Alexander, 45; work as secretary, 52, 93, 96, 164
Macdonald, Mr..(house painters), 103
Magna Charta, 2
Manchester, Bishop of, 33, 81
Manchester Bricklayers' Association, 118, 121

Mason, Hugh, 88
Masons, wages of, 8, 10; higher than other crafts because of "union," 11
Masters and servants, decisions on Acts relating to, 39 : law amended, 39, 167
Mill, J. S., 28, 39, 77, 129, 148
Millers, the, 171 (note)
Miners, condition of, 22, 33
Mines Regulation Act, 89
"Mistaken men," 109
Monasteries, dissolution of, 14
More's *Utopia*, 16
Morley, John, 72
Mundella, A. J., 88

N

Nasmyth, Mr., 153
Neale's, Mr., Bill, 36
New Zealand, trade unions in, 65
National Federation of Employers, 57
Non-producers, 134
Non-unionists profit by unionism, 84; refusing to work with, 84, 118
Normansell, Mr., 166
Norman Society, the, 26
Northumberland and Durham miners, 45

O

Odger, George, 115
Operative house painters, alliance of, 68
Outrages at Sheffield, 40

P

Paris, cabmen, 60; conference at, 61, 180; workman's wages in, 63

Paris, Comte de, 180
Paterson, Mrs., 116
Peasants' Revolt, the, 13
People, income of, 72
Petition *in re* Hornby *v.* Close, 38
Pickard, Mr., 92
Piccework, 90
Platt, Messrs., dispute with, 32, 46
Plimsoll, Samuel, 56
Poor laws, 18
"Poor Priests," Wiklif's, 12
Prices of coal and rates of wages, 75
Prior, J. D., 77
Profits, go to capitalists, 31

R

Railway servants, French and Belgian, 60
Rattening, 30
Recapitulation, 178
Repeal of the corn laws, effect of, 22
Rogers, Thorold, 4, 6, 7, 11, 22, 61, 162
Royal Commission, the, 35 (note), 41

S

Saddlers' combination suppressed, 11
Sale, Sir Robert, a serf, 12
Salmon and Scotch labourers, 7 (note)
Saunders, William, 40, 82 (note)
"Scamping," 161
Scotch bakers, the, 33
Scotch labourers and salmon, 7 (note).

Secretary of union, difficulties of his position, 92
Serfdom, 2; not yet abolished, 3
Serfs, 2; emancipation of, 3, 11
Sheffield outrages, the, 40
Shakespeare, alluded to, 2
Shipbuilders, the, 35
Shoemakers, imprisoned for combining, 11
Shopkeepers, help those on strike, 132
Short hours, effect of, 157
Simcox, Mr., 62
Smith, Adam, 89, 129
Socialism, 59, 152
Spitalfield weavers, 33
Statistics collected by unions, 176
Statutes of labourers, 5, 7, 15
Statutes referred to, 23 Edw. III. c. 1, 5; 37 Edw. III. c. 14, 7; 34 Edw. IV. c. 9, 11; 3 Hy. VI. c. 1, 11; 2 & 3 Edw. VI. c. 15, 15, 18; 22 & 23 Chas. II. 18; 6 Geo. IV. c. 129, 19; 13 Geo. IV. c. 68, 33
Strikes, assisted by shopkeepers, 132; benefit other trades, 84; care taken to prevent, 92, 93; decided by ballot, 54; at wrong times may prevent a rise, 95; in early days were numerous, 10; the first one, 6; money expended on, 55; prevented by trade unions, 102, 105; safeguards against, 53, 54; stimulate inventions, 153; "unsuccessful strikes succeed," 78. Strikes and lockouts referred to—Ashton and Stalybridge, 79; agricultural labourers, 81; bricklayers, 74; builders, 78, 79, 80; engineers, 47, 73, 77, 80; ironworkers, 80; Preston, 79; St. Helens and Wigan, 93;

spinners, 79; tailors, 80, 81, 100
Sumptuary laws, 7
Sunderland, disputes at, 47, 77

T

Tailors of London, the chief cloth importers, 4, 68, 80, 81, 100
Technical education, etc., 122, 158
Thornton, W. T., 27, 31, 44, 68, 80, 107, 112, 148
Towns, growth of, 5
Trade councils, 57
Trade unionism, growth of, 106; its unselfishness, 56; not a violation of free trade, 128; an ironmaster's opinion on, 162
Trade unions' congress, none but delegates take part at, 59 (note); functions and work of, 57
Trade unionists, sometimes refuse to work with non-unionists, 84; number of, 106; bad practices of, 123; are good workmen, 159; good character necessary for, 160; do not sacrifice their liberty, 174
Trade unions, the first, 26; their origin, 26; secret meetings of, 26; disguised as friendly societies, 27; founded on the old guilds, 27; early faults, 30; forced into existence, 32; attempts to crush, 34; first conference of delegates, 35; Bill to protect funds, 37; petition in re Hornby v. Close, 38; objects of, variously stated, 43; not solely protective, 44; their efficacy, 67; admitted by em-

ployers, 109; have raised wages, 68, *et seq.*; raise wages sooner, 75; cannot determine rate of wages, 141; help non-unionists, 84; sometimes err, 91; cannot cause strikes, 105; prevent them, 102; are not protectionists, 127; publicity of proceedings of, 122; women's unions, 115; "benefits," insurance, etc., 111; as friendly societies, 175; their influence, 126; as political educators, 164; collect statistics, 176; keep record of wages, 74, of prices, 94; make good citizens, 171; agitate for beneficent legislation, 165; bad rules in, 114, 118, 121; in New Zealand, 65; in France, 62

Truck system, the, 76 (note)

Tyler's rebellion, 13

U

Unequal laws, 35

Unionism, *see* trade unionism

Unionists, *see* trade unionists

Unions, *see* trade unions

Utopia, 16

V

Villeins, 2

W

Wages, enormous rise of, after black death, 8; masons', 8, 10; justices' power to fix, 18, 20; failure of attempts to regulate, 20; clothworkers', 20; fifty years ago, 70; lower where unions are not, 85; natural rate of, 94; must sometimes fall, 164; minimum rate of, 120; are always below value of work done, 75; high, effects of, 155; and the price of coal, 145, 146; of Paris workmen, 63

Wales, wages in, 69

Watchmakers' Society, the, 26

West Suffolk farmers, 97

Wiklif's "Poor Priests," 12

Wilcock, Mr., 158

Women's Protective and Provident League, 116, 117

Women's unions, 115

Woods, E., 55

Work, quality of, 161

Working class, formation of, 5; wages of, 5; halcyon days of, 8; decline of, 13, 21, 24

Working Men's Association, 35

Y

Yorkshire and Derbyshire coal-owners, 100

PRINTED BY WILLIAM CLOWES AND SONS, LIMITED, LONDON AND BECCLES.

www.ingramcontent.com/pod-product-compliance
Lightning Source LLC
Chambersburg PA
CBHW030836270326
41928CB00007B/1086